ASCENSION

AND

THE FIFTH DIMENSIONAL NETWORK

Andrew Smith and Keith Laidler

LIGHT OF AVALON BOOKS

Ascension and the Fifth Dimensional Network

Copyright 2012 Andrew Smith and Keith Laidler

Andrew Smith and Keith Laidler assert the moral right to be
identified as the authors of this work.

First published 2012

ISBN 978 0-9555312-2-4

A catalogue entry for this book is available from
the British Library

Cover illustration by Kevin Laidler

Book design and layout by Mike Cooter

Published in the UK by Light of Avalon Books

Distribution enquiries to:
Gazelle Book Services Ltd
www.gazellebooks.co.uk

Our website: www.fifthdimensionalnetwork.com

Printed in England by Digital Book Print

CONTENTS

Acknowledgement and dedication

Many heart-felt thanks to the Spiritual Master Quan Yin, who is indeed an "Angel of Compassion" and so much more. We acknowledge her inspired hand in and around all the understandings and realities described in the chapters following.

We further are most grateful to the "Management Team" of Masters Quan Yin, El Morya, Rakoczy, Kuthumi and Archangel Michael for sharing the genius of their inter dimensional programme for interested members of humanity to move to the Fifth Dimensional New Earth – the Golden Age so many have dreamed about. This Gift from God now being offered is commended to all those readers who have maintained their faith in a joyful and love-based world, despite often extreme challenges in their current lives in the current third dimensional world.

Thanks and appreciation to Robert Mulliss of the Wessex Research Group for his help and support in the production of this work.

Introduction

At the time of writing in late May 2012, we have completed publication on the Internet of the series of six articles from Quan Yin and El Morya in the series entitled "The Ascension Opportunity of 2011/12 (www.revolutionof2012.net). With equal intent, we have opened the new website "The Fifth Dimensional Network (Dnet) (www.fifthdimesionalnetwork.com), which contains all the available descriptions and instructions for the Dnet brought into being through the sterling efforts of Keith Laidler. Additional chapters have been added specifically explaining the vital role of the Dnet at this time in facilitating the human evolution to the Fifth Dimensional (5D) New Earth, for those who choose to make the move.

The El Morya chapters are specifically credited as such. The remainder of the material originated from Quan Yin.

Most of the population of industrialised English-speaking countries have regular access to these websites through the internet. However, the Spiritual Management team for both the Dnet and the Earth's Ascension have stipulated that a book version containing all the material posted on the Dnet website is needed in addition to allow this body of information to be accessed as desired by those without internet access.

In preparing this edition, we have added some additional perceptions and understandings. These will enable the reader to observe on the one hand the human needs arising out of the Earth's Ascension to Fifth Dimensional Consciousness. In the second part, one can see these needs being addressed and fully met through the invitation to join the Dnet and becoming aligned with its dynamic pre-formed energy structure.

It is suggested that the best place to start is to digest the comprehensive description of the Earth's Ascension process set out in the Quan Yin/ElMorya articles. They provide a high level of briefing about what is going on with the Earth's Ascension from the Management Team responsible for its successful implementation. They offer guidance as to how humanity might best interact with that process for their highest good.

The Dnet's qualities and built-in resources reassuringly address all the concerns they might have about going through the Ascension and thriving in the process. Of course, it is not necessary on a practical level to fully understand what the Earth and all her inhabitants are faced with during the Earth's Ascension to 5D Consciousness in order to deeply engage with the extraordinary facilities built into the Dnet – although it would help somewhat.

In fact, it is not necessary to absolutely believe in the Earth's Ascension to greatly benefit from membership of the Dnet and its uplifting energy structure. It is highly probable though that all those individuals drawn to take part in the Dnet will have indeed noticed many of the changes taking place on the planet physically, in the quality of etheric energy now accessible by humans and in the breaking down of major social and economic institutions.

It is not essential for them to understand and believe in all the many ramifications of what is an extraordinarily complex multi-dimensional process. It is unlike anything previously in the history of the Earth going back millions of years, let alone the modest level of happenings within your individual lifetimes.

The reasons for joining the Dnet are set out clearly and cogently in Part II of this book and it is strongly suggested that the reader joins the Dnet directly after finishing the book and experience the energy for themselves. In the unlikely event that you do not wish to continue after evaluating the Dnet for several weeks, you only need to state that you are leaving and there will be no further interaction.

There is definitely no risk in "trying on" the energy structure and "seeing how it fits". The probability is that your enhanced perception and healing ability, the opening to a high vibration community as part of the 5D New Earth, coupled with firm protection from any challenges from the darker side of existence, will provide you with great satisfaction and a joyful life fulfilment.

Raising the consciousness level at which one engages with life can open the doors to many higher aspects of experiences and situations. These would be a great boon in themselves for enjoying a more creative and expressive life – even if the Earth was not in the process of making a major dimensional shift. You are warmly invited to share this magnificent journey.

PART ONE:

THE ASCENSION OPPORTUNITY OF 2011/12

CHAPTER ONE
A Vision of Life on the New Earth

The period that humanity is going through as a great collective group is immense. Here and there some guidelines of explanation are being circulated about what's happening. They are being read by a few people and understood by even fewer. With so many busy activities being required of most individuals in physical form, it is challenging to keep track of the key essence of each day, the truth which is there. And yet the situation is such that you need to rise to that challenge of maintaining and extending your understanding each day.

It's like there is a new dish or almost new menu being presented by the Spiritual Hierarchy to each of you when you wake up in the morning hours. It is almost as if the world is being re-programmed in the small hours on a nightly basis, although there are not any signs up saying so, let alone major notifications in the mass media. One of the objectives of this communication is just to say it as clearly as possible – "Each day is becoming more and more different from its predecessor than you have ever experienced".

Taking a broad view, this is very much in the category of "Good News" for those within humanity who have aspired to a much more harmonious life on the Earth — a life where things work out well and lovingly as a normal feature of engagement with other people and all the other dimensions of Livingness, where every activity in which you engage has a built-in joyfulness. Millions have aspired at various times to be part of such a world – a rather smaller number are still holding that belief and truth within their hearts currently.

So this message is for those of you who have voyaged successfully to this point, on the eve of a gargantuan change, with your heart's aspirations intact. We are going to show you a place you've not been to before, or at least not for a very long time.

Ascension and the Fifth Dimensional Network

Let us envisage a beautiful grassy valley – a shallow valley rather than one with steep sides – dotted with wild flowers, with a variety of quite mature trees as well as some younger ones. There is a small river, more the size of a brook perhaps, running along the base of the valley, twisting and turning as is the way of running water – knowing where it has to go in the end, staying with its course.

There are several comfortable wooden benches near the brook of the sort that have curved wooden backs, so that you are fully supported. You find yourself looking around at this beautiful valley – the air is full of the deepest fragrances. In the background you hear a great diversity of joy-filled birds singing from their hearts. Sunlight radiates continuously with a gentle temperature. While you're taking in the whole scene here, you are invited to sit down on one of these most comfortable benches, still surrounded by this total beauty. So please do that now.

You become aware of a new rhythm flowing through your body – it comes up through your feet, up through your ankles, through your legs to your hips, into the abdominal area, flowing up the spine, filling the chest , moving up through the neck to fill the head, down the arms also.

Then you notice the change in frequency – a pulsing energy. You notice outside that the colours in the sky appear to be in synchronicity with these energies you feel pulsing upwards through your body. In some way, the colours and shades are moving in accordance with this pulsing energy within you. Even the birdsong changes and joins in this unified expression. You feel wave after wave of this joy-filled energy.

With so many overlapping frequencies, you see a kaleidoscope of colours changing each fraction of a second. As you sit there, you are totally part of this experience of vibrant life energy. It's like you are immersed in the deepest music yet it's a music without notes – tiny pulses, thousands of them, producing harmonies beyond anything you have ever heard previously. Within your mind, colours come and go in tune with these musical impulses. You are truly at one with all the energies of this enchanted valley.

Now you are invited to choose a thought related to one of your deepest aspirations. Bring this thought and aspiration into your mind and hold it there lovingly. Then see it very gently extending down to your heart centre, so that it exists strongly in both areas. As you embrace this aspirational thought, it develops some structure, taking on some kind of texture.

You notice that the energy flow within your body seems to have reversed. Instead of the energy flow coming up through your feet, your power is coming instead from aspirational thought, that related to your new creation. It seems to flow downward through the legs, out through the feet out into the valley. It begins to take form in this magical place because you are at one with the whole valley, its inhabitants and all its energetic patterns and frequencies.

And so all life in the valley responds to your new creation. Although the birds singing are still themselves, they respond by putting out their higher vibrational patterns in perfect alignment with your new creation. The murmurs and the bubbling sounds from the brook also change to harmonise with your creative energies now spreading throughout the whole valley.

You can even feel the trees as Great Spirits, smiling as they give their energies also towards the manifestation of your creation. For them it is second nature to respond in this way. Within the rays of the Sun, you notice there the change of emphasis also, an overtone difference, it seems.

You see and feel your creation coming into a visible etheric form, one that you can feel clearly, gradually becoming more visible. You notice that the energy is still flowing from your head and heart continuously and steadily, going out into the valley, finding its way to all the parts it needs to go – to bring this creation into fruition.

The Extraordinary Adjustment Required to Reach 5D

This is an important glimpse, or vision if you prefer, of the creation process used by the Divine Feminine in its many activities within your Earth as well as in many other places within the Universe. We are bringing this understanding to your attention to help in this huge adjustment that individuals on Earth are currently facing, even those who have been on the Spiritual Path for many years. They are facing this enormous adjustment to much higher levels of consciousness, which are opening up at an exponential rate.

At these higher levels of consciousness, the abilities to create and manifest are unlimited to an extraordinary extent, compared with what you are familiar with in the 3rd and 4th dimensions of consciousness. The old saying "Be careful what you wish for because it may come true" is going to be amplified in its importance some 1,000 times. Your creation will begin to come into being almost immediately you envisage it, which can be a most joyful way of living – a joyful experience once you have mastered the very necessary degree of self-discipline. Without this self-discipline, it can be, shall we say, an exciting ride down the rapids of one of your rushing mountain rivers. Since some people choose to do that for fun, it's not a terrible thing in itself, provided you have trained yourself for that kind of experience. Otherwise it can lead to difficult consequences.

We are planting this understanding and now bringing it to the forefront of your attention so that you have the opportunity to work with it, play with it, internalise it a little before you find it is the normal way of operating in the New Earth. This will enable you to proceed through relatively calm waters.

So now you can see your creation before you – it's yours! You can return to this valley by just using the name Quan Yin to call on me. The right level, from which I am speaking now, will respond, as you keep the picture of the valley in your mind. The whole process starts and moves forward – we have created it that way.

So there is plenty of homework here and we are looking at a transition to this much higher level of consciousness within days and weeks, although the Gregorian calendar does not really relate very precisely. It is more likely to happen in stages –rather irregular stages – with sudden surges of energy around one particular aspect and then, perhaps, another balancing inflow from another angle. We do guarantee that you will wake up each morning, from now on, feeling quite different from how you felt the previous day, even though you may have to encounter some of the same people – yet they will not seem quite the same. Sometimes they may seem to be significantly different as they themselves move forwards on their Path of Evolution.

The one outcome you can depend on is that the whole process of creating the New Earth will move forward to the complete manifestation of its designed framework and energy flow.

Balance, Harmony and Stillness Within

As we move forward into this world which responds so directly and harmoniously to the procedures of inspired creation already outlined, it is vital to maintain a methodical meticulousness as to how your thoughts, feelings, beliefs and aspirations are allowed to go out into the world of New Earth. There is not going to be the "fail-safe" buffer of time delay and resistance, with which we are used to interacting in the third dimensional world.

The new set-up is both exciting and demanding for each individual human who opens to the opportunity of Ascension to these realms of higher Fifth Dimensional Consciousness. Without this "fail-safe" buffer of inertia, and without the complex pattern of motivations and constraints from your individual karmic package, creative energy from your heart-centre manifests into Fifth Dimensional structures without let or hindrance. And your creation (and its successors) will inherently contain the harmony, inter-dependence and joyful co-operation of the New Earth.

With that degree of creative ability available, a person may well wish to practice being absolutely still in both mind and heart-centre as a normal "state of being". This is then the starting point when a creative design needs to be worked on actively and then manifested. It's rather like switching off your car engine when the vehicle has no need to move forwards or backwards. In this way, when the creation faculty is engaged, it is not going to be mixed up with a multitude of other thoughts and feelings from other projects and/or contexts.

Whether you are in a male or female body, it is essential to develop the inner feminine because that is the source of your individual creative ability and power to manifest desired outcomes. So in the White Brotherhood mystery schools during the last several thousand years, a female initiate learned the inner power of masculine projection, while a male initiate had to master both feminine receptiveness deep within their body as well as learning to use the power of projection from the integrated mind and heart-centre.

As you welcome each day within this intense stage of the Earth's journey of Ascension, you are invited to feel and inhale the new energy of the day upon awakening. In this way, you will be most able to appreciate the very real unfolding of the Fifth Dimensional Consciousness and the birth of your New World, as part of the New Earth.

Ascension Opportunities for Families and Friends

One of the many challenges built into this process is that each person Ascending needs to lovingly come to terms with the understanding that Ascension is an individual Spiritual process. Family connections, friendship patterns and other inter-relationships may be strong in the third and fourth dimensional worlds. However, once the karmic energies pulling individuals together in one-on-one or group partnerships have been fulfilled into neutrality (a condition of Ascension to Fifth Dimensional Consciousness), the remaining "heart to heart" relationship related energy flows may not require a continuing daily interaction. The phrase "love you always" will take on a new meaning at the Fifth Dimensional level, as it will be straightforward to send and receive loving energy at a heart level indefinitely, without the third and fourth dimensional need for close physical proximity.

Naturally, each parent who individually commits themselves and prepares for Ascension also wishes that their children will ascend in similar fashion. But whether or not a child is ready and willing to move up to a radically new dimension at this time is determined by the child's Higher Self, rather than by family loyalties and perceived obligations.

The love and protective instincts of the parent can best be expressed by advising/briefing each child about what the Earth's Ascension means for them, in whatever terminology works in the context of that child's level of development and the particular parent/child relationship. The parent can also send higher frequency energy to the child as a kind of "homing signal", which the child may or may not use to raise their consciousness.

Ultimately the child's Higher Self and the Lords of Karma will have the final say on whether the child is ready for the Ascension to Fifth Dimensional Consciousness or whether they need to experience one or more further lifetimes on an available planet still at the third/fourth dimensional level. We all knew before we incarnated into the current lifetime what were the patterns of possibilities and probabilities within our destiny pattern and the degree of opportunity to Ascend to the Fifth Dimensional New Earth. Then the exercise of freewill by the individual determines the pathways of experience and the outcomes within the karmic patterns of destiny.

The older the child, the less influence the parent can bring to bear (no surprises there). Every child who has completed the first 13 years is Spiritually an adult, whatever their ongoing needs for support and nurturing. The children under 13 are more susceptible to the parental influence and more able to follow a parental Ascension, if that is happening.

The love and caring an adult individual feels for other adults, whether they be partners, friends or relatives, can also be expressed by the advising/briefing process about the rapidly approaching Ascension opportunity, should that other adult be open to hearing and responding – obviously a freewill decision. But an enlightened adult can certainly send higher frequency energy to the other person in a "homing signal" role, which can make a real difference in Ascension outcome in borderline cases.

Help in Moving Forwards is Readily Available

Feel free to implement any and all of these practices in these vital days prior to the Earth's completing its Ascension to Fifth Dimensional Consciousness. You may call on me by name (Quan Yin) for help and insight in making your own preparations to move forwards and upwards.

CHAPTER TWO
The Values and Energy Structures
of the New Earth

Your world is moving closer to the brink of financial collapse. Concurrently, the great Earth Being you know as Gaia is moving further towards the culmination of her Ascension to Fifth Dimensional Consciousness (5D). This is most certainly a time when a wise student on the Spiritual Path pays attention to the practical provisions for your family's physical support during this time of transition, along with the attunement to the higher levels of consciousness which will enable you to be part of the 5D New Earth. The old 3D Earth is in the process of being released by Gaia and will end up as a somewhat inert mass, quite similar to the current 3D Mars.

An important part of the day to day preparations to come through these challenging times marking the final implosion of a rotted societal structure, is to learn to co-operate far more closely with like-minded individuals. By forming groups and examining in detail what it would be like to live together in community, you are coalescing a powerful energetic vibration which will facilitate your stepping into a higher consciousness of existence. You more clearly recognise the priority of a service-to-others orientation in your life, phasing out any past pre-occupations with self-gratification.

This co-operation and movement towards closely shared life experiences is of the utmost value and relevance for surviving the decline and failure of supply/distribution systems for the basic necessities of life. But it can also facilitate the first steps of bringing 5D energies into your daily experience and beginning to incorporate them into your lives on a more permanent basis.

The Ascension of the Earth to 5D marks her re-entry into her family of planets within your Solar System and an end to her hitherto separation. For the human individuals living on her surface, there is a corresponding change from the isolated person exercising their freewill "to obtain what they want" to a more enlightened being attuned to higher consciousness and sharing the joys of living with those all around them. This fundamental shift is well underway and there's no way it's ever going into reverse. The old 3D Earth will go into relative oblivion, without either lifeforce or human inhabitants.

Going Beyond the Limitations of Self-Gratification

So a committed community group can move towards a deeper integration by sharing their lives week by week on a grounded physical level, with plenty of opportunities for mutual service, support and real caring. They can also come together to learn and practise the attunement with higher consciousness, which will facilitate their passage to 5D and subsequently living on the New Earth.

Our introduction in the previous chapter, to the creation process of 5D living, illustrated the unlimited possibilities and potential when you have broad access to the Divine power, coupled with a joyful harmony and alignment with all the other living beings in your vicinity. By maintaining this continuous alignment, you avoid the almost inevitable opposition to any creative proposal put together on 3D Earth, stemming from the absence of shared values and understanding. Without any sense of loving consideration, this results in a morass of rivalry, destructive competition, power plays etc.

Within what is loosely termed the "New Age" movement, there is a very great need to step beyond self-gratification, self-aggrandisement and other expressions of ego, which impede (often severely) the opening up of a love-based Spiritual attunement. These are fundamental requirements if you want to grow towards the 5D consciousness of the New Earth. Instead of a person priding themselves on how much more they know and understand compared with their peers, a love-based individual (with a sense of shared camaraderie) will find often subtle ways to share the insights which have helped them develop a higher perception of human life, and the etheric realms.

At the 5D level of the New Earth, an individual's experience of living is like being part of dozens of communities simultaneously. It is vital that an individual has developed a strong inner sense of self, along with a clear mind, before precipitating themselves into this multi-dimensional arena.

At the 3D level, an individual has the opportunity to go deeper into each situation, event, relationship and/or challenge, because things do not happen simultaneously. They also do not happen instantaneously, so there is time and space to address the individual components of a situation, as Master Rakoczy has explained in the context of using the Violet Flame (www.revolutionof2012.net — Sparkford School of Spiritual Mysteries).

Replacing Old Patterns as you Move to 5D

A major task for a Spiritually inclined individual, on the eve of the Earth's Ascension, is to find alternative ways of living within each day. In this way every endeavour at work, at home or in developing co-operative undertakings with friends and fellow travellers on the Path, can become at least a partial replica of the energy patterns awaiting you at the 5D level.

This new approach requires an ongoing self-monitoring to identify, challenge and replace old 3D patterns of thinking, speaking, hearing and taking action, with attributes of a 5D essence. Then each day you can certify that you have advanced to a higher level in terms of these "nuts and bolts" of interacting with life itself. The key values of love, compassion, empathy, clarity of perception, focused actions and creativity are integrated into each moment – all these require the initiate to be fully engaged with their incorporation into daily living.

Alongside your personal endeavours, our team from the Divine Feminine will work with each of you every day (and even more at night) to raise your vibration directly through the impregnation of higher frequencies. These will be selected to be in accordance with the advancing refinement of the Earth's vibratory lifeforce and, simultane-

23

ously, to be of a level that you can absorb harmoniously, maintaining a functioning balance with the place you reached the previous day.

We offer this personalised intervention with a full understanding and recognition of the great effects it will have on each individual who has the courage and determination to ask for this help. You need to be sure in yourself that you really want to complete the evolutionary stage of 3D living and move up to the next class level of 5D.

At this juncture, it is not an opportunity which you can "try before you buy", let alone decide halfway up the ladder of Ascension that living at a much higher vibration is "not what you really want to do." You either commit fully to Ascend or stay at your current paradigm. And we have built in the safety measure that, if you are not ready for this great leap forward, you will not feel drawn to seek our help and involvement.

If you decide that you are sure that you wish to participate in this Ascension process, then you call on me by name Quan Yin and state in plain language that you wish to engage with and take part in our programme. You then need to make a personal commitment to self-monitor yourself continually and move towards the 5D pattern as previously described. You can count on our response and enfoldment.

It will be beneficial for individuals, who have made this commitment to Ascend, to get together regularly to attune to the 5D energies in a meditative state. We are making our recording of the 5D creation process available to act as a reliable tuning signal. Invoking the Quan Yin energy directly is also effective, as we respond by flooding the room with 5D energies to be taken in and absorbed.

Going Beyond Physical Communities to the Golden Path

At an initial stage of our plans for humanity at this time of the Earth's Ascension, we envisaged the formation of physical communities, akin to self-contained villages, to provide a beneficial framework which we would use for Spiritual enhancement of the community members. By living together in one location, there would be a multitude of opportunities for individuals to grow by loving service to the greater whole. With enough commitment and cooperation to achieve community objectives, the whole enterprise could be elevated to the 5D level.

Some have asked why these planned communities never really manifested at a physical level. We have observed that each individual, who expressed interest in joining a community, was targeted by negative energies, which abound in the astral planes surrounding the Earth at a 3D level. This is nothing new – the course of human life on Earth has been described by the Hermetic (Hermes Trismegistus) as the "University of the Negative". His teaching emphasised learning about positive-negative polarity and learning to recognise what is going on within each situation.

Each student within this paradigm has had to either develop a deep inner strength and focused will, with which to move forward with their life endeavours, or become overwhelmed and fall back. The power of the negative forces at this critical stage reached unforeseen levels and only a few would-be founders of these communities had their resolution unaffected by the onslaught.

It became clear that the community energy and framework, which we had envisaged, was blocked at the 5D level because of the opposition running rampant at the 3D level. This phenomenon had also occurred at the conclusion of the Atlantean experiment, when the remaining land was sinking, and we were addressing alternative ways of living. Then there was all the derision heaped upon gallant Noah, while he prepared by building his Ark.

It is at the end of such an era (or cataclysmic cycle) that we provide for a splitting of the dimensions through which humans are evolving. This happened at the end of Atlantis and it is happening now. This provision is described fully in Vol. 2 of The Revolution of 2012 and it's how things are – it's what is available. The Golden Path takes the committed student to 5D and provides protection from diversions and distractions of all kinds.

The key to your most positive evolution and your ascent along the Golden Path is your personal decision to join the Ascension journey or go your own way. It is up to you to make a conscious choice looking with open awareness at the opportunity being presented.

Should you desire further assistance, feel free to contact Andrew Smith, who is available for us to communicate through to bring our message and energy to you, your friends and/or your group during the months to come.

CHAPTER THREE
El Morya: Making Your Personal Ascension a Priority

The Spiritual Hierarchy, of which the White Brotherhood is a part, has worked comprehensively to lead, guide and support the Ascension of the Great Spirit of the Earth (Gaia if you will) to Fifth Dimensional Consciousness (5D). We have gone to great lengths to help those members of humanity, who have ears to hear, to wake up to the full implications of the Earth's Ascension for those currently incarnated on the surface of the planet.

The Importance of Daily Focus

We have noticed that, while quite a number of Spiritual aspirants would welcome the new experience and conditions of living at 5D, only a modest number are giving their personal Ascension a priority within their current choices for each day – unfolding into weeks and months.

The vital understanding about making your personal Ascension be part of the New World and New Earth being created, is that it requires each aspiring individual to affirm each day their ongoing wish to make this vast transition. In the Revolution of 2012 Vol. 2, you have been taught about the separation of the two diverging paths. You have learnt about the magical power that has been created in the Golden Path to enable the genuine aspirant to go through the necessary initiatory processes, that we have established for you, to attune to this great leap in planetary consciousness.

Now is the time to focus on this process of connecting to enable each Initiate to be fully at the level required for them to be within the 5D energy, while being able to function as a balanced individual. The experience of being exposed to the refined 5D energetic vibrations and power, while still being individually at a 3D or 4D level is not recommended. Terms like "shock" and "overwhelming" apply.

Following Spiritual Guidance and Directions

The popular "New Age" belief that one can just float up to the required level without doing the specified work is a major misunderstanding. It would be like going to a major London railway terminus and just getting on the first train which took your fancy (like priorities and/or indulgence within the day) in the expectation that you will get to the 5D world anyway.

In fact the process is much closer to Harry Potter's initial experience at Kings Cross station, where he had to pass through a brick wall in order to find himself in the alternative reality from which the train to the wizard's school was waiting to depart. Harry fortunately listened to the guidance of how to pass through the brick wall and was open to meeting the special requirements of his journey to Hogwarts. Had he not been willing to take in the instructions and then project himself towards the brick wall, he would have stayed within the constraints of his prior reality.

For most of you, the Ascension to 5D will be of no less magnitude than Harry's leap into the unknown. If you listen to the guidelines and follow what is required, we in the White Brotherhood along with the Angelic Realms, will make sure you move up the Golden Path to 5D. But we need you to "sign on" in terms of your overt commitment and clear affirmation daily that you want to make this extraordinary journey. If you have questions about what to do, feel free to ask us directly and/or through Andrew Smith.

We have been asked repeatedly about the timing of all aspects of the Earth's transition to 5D: when the physical earth changes are happening, when Gaia will have completed her transition to 5D etc. Unfortunately, the Gregorian calendar and its units of timing do not fit the various combinations of markers that the Spiritual Hierarchy use to record progress towards a multidimensional evolutionary goal.

However, when all the "ducks" are lined up in a row, it will all unfold swiftly.

Comparison with Ecological Change

Rather than worrying about being able to forecast the unforecastable, we suggest you take on board the realisation that, when Gaia has energetically reached 5D, there will no longer be life-support energy available for humans and other lifeforms still attuned to 3D and 4D levels. It will be just like you see in Nature when there is a substantial ecological change in the growing conditions available: maybe temperature and/or humidity, rainfall, sunlight etc. Without the required combination of conditions, the plants and trees cease to function and just fade away.

There is no judgement of any aspect of these species departing being in some way "right or wrong" – it's just that conditions changed. It is the natural way. For individual humans, choosing not to do what is necessary to make this arch-transition of Ascension, they will find it impossible to sustain their old life on Earth. They will move on to other planets which are available for all who wish to continue with the curriculum of 3D and 4D. Just like within a school structure, students only pass on to a higher grade when they have completed their various studies in the previous classes.

Whatever your decisions, implicit or explicit, know that our love for all humanity is eternal, even as different parts of the species evolve in their own time to higher levels of life expression.

CHAPTER FOUR
The Ascension Opportunity for Humanity

In our two previous expositions, we have drawn your attention to how different are the energies comprising Fifth Dimensional (5D) Consciousness on the most practical level, let alone how they are on the higher aspects of the esoteric. We have shown you the extreme degree of interconnectedness of all life forms, although these are only "extreme" when looked at from the point of view of Earth's third dimensional 3D level.

From the perspective of the 5D level of consciousness, it seems absolutely normal that all life forms co-operate with each other, generously support each others' needs and their new endeavours. However, given the current situation which exists with humanity and the surface of the Earth in general, we realise that this is quite a big step-up in both understanding and consciousness. In a society where competition and rivalry, along with the use of the sharp elbow, are normal ways of going through the day, it is indeed a massive change that is required of any individual who desires to be part of the New Earth.

The Evolutionary Plan for the Whole Solar System

We wish for you and encourage you to make the effort to be part of this transition, which the wise ones on Earth have looked forward to for tens of thousands of years. This is not something which has just popped up in the last few years or, indeed, in the last few decades – its part of a great evolutionary plan for the whole Solar System.

The other planets made their transitions quite some time ago, leaving behind their 3D experience. Yet the Earth (Gaia if you like) chose to stay at this more basic level for her own reasons – for her own evolution as she perceived it then, as was her right to do so.

Because the planetary interaction within your solar system is so interconnected, the absence of the Earth participating has been causing more and more distortions within the operation of your Solar System. Although some of your planets like Jupiter have evolved considerably further than 5D level, others have had to stay down because of their closer connections with the Earth. This interconnectedness is not just a handy phrase or a "nice to have" feeling – this is about the very lifeblood of the Solar System, the flow of energy between and around the Sun and her planets. It is vital to have the Earth participating at a similar level as the planets still at 5D level.

The Earth (Gaia) has come to realise all this and is now moving very fast in her own Ascension to catch up, after a rather slow start. This has made the challenge for humanity a lot more substantial – with the planet herself being very tardy, it has seemed much less urgent for humans to consider making this evolutionary step.

There are so many other things to do in your Western society. We do not need to call them "distractions" as there is always a validity in all the actions which humans choose to do, while they're incarnated in these magnificent and beautifully designed bodies. It is not all that surprising, given the on-going need of the human subconscious mind to continually re-create past conditions, until it's told to do something better.

Humans are finding it so difficult to wake up to the urgency of their individual need to change the way they are focusing and prioritising, changing the way they are approaching each day, each week and each month. The life energies are not the same as they were last year and definitely not the same as the year before that. The rate of change is closer to an exponential rise in energetic consciousness. But there is no big sign up in the sky saying so. There are very few individuals who are fully conscious of the speed of this Ascent – we wish it were otherwise.

Explaining to Others about the Earth's Ascension

Well, this is a long explanation why at this particular moment in time we are asking those of you who have some understanding of the situation facing humanity to find the courage and communication skills to put out this message, in the very best way you can, to those around you. We know that, given the lack of consciousness of many of them, it is not the easiest thing to get across.

But, as an expression of caringness you have for those close to you, those around you and those you interact with, we seriously ask and suggest that you take the bit between your teeth and make an effort to find ways to plant a few seeds in other people's understandings, however many times that you have tried that in the past and been disappointed or felt rebuffed, as you've experienced people not responding.

You, as individuals, are getting stronger each day so we are asking you to have the courage to use that new strength to take a few risks in communication. This may be what you do not want to hear. It is not an easy thing to approach even those who believe that they are "on the Spiritual Path" as well as those who believe they are within the New Age generation of people, who have taken at least a somewhat alternative approach to life.

We do not underestimate the determination that it took to individually go down one of the roads much less travelled than the mainstream. But there is not an awful lot of time left so, for the sake of those you care for, try and get some understanding across. Sometimes, talking or working-in some understandings about the "heart-opening" can be something that people can hear without being too shocked.

Getting Ready for the Higher Frequencies of 5D

Opening the Heart-Centre is a vital foundation. In addition it is absolutely necessary that each individual has to have had at least a little experience of these higher vibrations of the 5D New Earth so that they actually know what they feel like. They need to have had a chance to incorporate them within your body's musical repertoire of all the notes, tones and chords with which it is familiar.

You have to add these higher expressions of sound and every other sort of vibration. So as the Earth finally breaks through to her full 5D level and the whole of the surface of the planet is flooded with this beautiful energy as it is, then some humans at least have the chance not to be overwhelmed by its immensity. A little experience beforehand can make all the difference.

We are focusing in these next months — as a planning framework if you like – to have groups taking place in different areas where we can introduce this energy, these extra vibrations. We can do this formally or informally but we do need to be invited along in some form. The group needs to be capable of listening, of creating a space within themselves to hear these new vibrations, this new "music".

Another challenging concept, which we are working hard to get across to humanity, is that as the Earth ascends to her 5D level, the old 3D planet Earth remains in existence. This is just like the old 3D "hulk" of what your scientists say remains of Mars. This is the counterpart of the current 5D planet with its thriving population. It's not that the 3D Earth in a matter of weeks suddenly becomes 5D. The 5D Earth actually opens out of the original planet, rather like an astral body separating from a physical body.

So choose to be part of the 5D Earth as it opens out – we're trying to show this to you visually – this etheric image pulling out of the rather dense physical 3D Earth that you know so well. But, if you individually wish to go with the higher-vibration version, you have to register and sign on, you have to exercise some will and say "That's the version and level I want to be connected to".

As you may have heard a number of times already, the 3D Earth is a freewill zone. This is quite different from planets at a 5D level and upwards as, within these more advanced societies, there is an instinctive understanding within each person of what they need to work and focus on – and so they naturally do what is needed, with great joy and great satisfaction. It is not that they do not have any freedom of choice – it is just that they continually choose to exercise their freedom by doing what is needed by the Godforce, the Living Spirit.

Meanwhile, down at 3D level on physical Earth, people do whatever they feel like, depending on how much they are separated from the "Greater Goodness". So when it comes to the splitting of the dimensions — the 5D Earth pulling away from the old 3D residue (or hulk) — humans wanting to be part of the 5D version, to be part of the New Earth with everything that implies, need to say and affirm every day that they do indeed want that.

We are not asking you in anyway to reject all the things that you have valued from your experience of living on the "old 3D Earth". You would not be the individuals you are if you had not had some positive experiences, recognising and being involved with the beauty that does exist on this "old version". A key realisation is that all that beauty is moving to be part of the New Earth also. It is not that you are losing any refined part of what you valued in the earlier, denser version of Earthness. That refined part is going up to 5D also and will be able to expand to even higher levels of beauty and illumination. We are inviting humanity — every person — to make the transition also.

Individuals who Uphold the Light

We recognise that at this time only a very modest number of individuals have any awareness of what is happening. This situation was not what we were working towards, it was not what we were envisaging, but we always knew it was a possibility, given the way humanity has been going.

In the last 2,000 years particularly, the battle between positive and negative has tilted somewhat towards the negative series of outcomes. Throughout this difficult period, there have always been those who upheld the Light during whatever challenge has been presented and we salute them for that. Those of you who hear this message of today we regard as part of that special group of human individuals who have upheld the Light, in this lifetime particularly. You knew this when you reincarnated at the beginning of this life – you knew that you had a special role to play. The fact that you have reached this moment here in this room today (or have otherwise made your commitment to be involved) is validation that you have not forgotten, you are still aware of this major part of your life purpose.

And your expression of your life purpose needs to be very strongly orientated to this great act of service in helping others wake up to the truth of what's happening now. We are not asking you to do it on your own. We have set up the energy structures so that, if you call upon us for help or assistance, we can be there quite directly, whether or not you can feel the presence of our team. That awareness sometimes needs repetition – a number of different experiences before you open up to internalise the energy which is being presented to you.

We would like to see groups opening up in other areas in addition to Somerset, Shropshire and Hampshire, where these are happening already. There is only a certain amount we can do from our side. The 3D Earth's energy structure has been put together so that souls who reincarnate here can choose, if they want, to be completely disconnected from the Spiritual Realms, as we live and know them.

Many souls in successive generations have chosen to make that disconnection to discover what it is like and continue to do so until some, at last, reach the point of saying: "Hmmm, there may be something in the other ways of living and doing things". Then gradually they can find their way back and begin the process of reconnecting to Spirit.

Life and Death Transitions and the New Earth

In one sense there is all eternity for that process to continue but there is not "all eternity" if you want to stay on the same planet. The Earth is moving up now and, if you want to take a lot more of "all eternity" to complete this process of moving away from connection to Spirit and then in your own time coming back again to reconnect, then you will need to do it on another planet, of which there are a number currently available. They may not be as beautiful as the Earth but they function adequately at a third and fourth dimensional level.

That's the best response if people ask "Well, what's going to happen to all those people who don't sign on to make this transition or don't want to do what's necessary to reach the 5D attunement"? These people can continue to take time to just work out their evolution as it unfolds – they just need to be on other planets to do so.

It is one of the obsessions within modern humanity – the fear and misunderstanding around death. Within the Ancient Wisdoms, the teachers going back thousands of years have always said "There is no death". In fact, the Spirit leaving the body is often a very joyful experience for the Spirit, for they realise that they are part of a wonderful Light existence and energy structure.

What is often not yet fully understood is that, as the physical body begins to change after the Spirit has left, its life energy just goes into other forms. You may have seen in some country churchyards how there are beautiful trees that are transforming the energy from the physical bodies that are buried there. They transform it into a whole new lifeform, as their roots pull all the nutrients from the formerly human body that is no longer needed by its previous user – the Spirit who graduated.

Now we are not holding our breath that humanity is suddenly going to change its misunderstandings around death, but it does help if those who are working with the Light do fully understand the process themselves. Sometimes if you witness somebody passing over, you can glimpse this joy.

Other teachings describe how death in this realm is regarded as a birth on the other side, as the Spirit comes back into the Spiritual Realms – so it's a joyful event. And from the point of view of the Spiritual Realms it's a bit of a death when you go and reincarnate in this rather variable experience known as being "alive on Earth". It's just a relative framework of observation and understanding.

But it is really helpful for your own understanding if you are trying to come to terms with this yourself about what happens to people who don't make this big transition to 5D Earth, the New Earth that's forming. None of this process involves the permanent cessation of a particular human being, an event around which humans might reasonably have some emotions.

We are talking about being able to accept that some humans incarnated in their bodies at the present time really have not got a clue about what is going on. It's about accepting that some other humans incarnated have a potential still to come to understand and realise what is going on with regard to the Earth's Ascension, and still make a connection to it. These are just different perspectives on the same actual event.

Maintaining Calm within the Storm

The growing turbulence in the energy on the surface of the Earth is going to continue to increase during these next months. We are aware that this is particularly challenging for you as individuals, who are attuned to the Light and a higher Spiritual Reality, despite everything that you have already coped with in your lives to date. We recognise that in these turbulent times that it needs a great expression of Will for you to maintain the necessary equilibrium and balance, so you can be some kind of working example to those around you.

But that is exactly why it is so important that you do so: to maintain some sense of calmness, of joyfulness, of a practical creativity, while having the ability to empathise with what those around you in the street, in your social circles, with your work associates, even with those you meet in the shops or with service providers. All those you come in touch with are going to be challenged to the core by the physical and societal turbulence, as the Earth moves higher and higher at a somewhat unreasonable speed, but it is what she has to do anyway.

So we are offering once more our assistance on a daily basis or more frequently – by the hour if necessary – to help each of you to stabilise and maintain equilibrium, whatever the external circumstances. We are not underestimating some of the situations you will be presented with, or have already been presented with and have had to find a way through them. The only way you can go seriously astray is by not asking for Spiritual help from the broad Spiritual Hierarchy. We're not just talking about Quan Yin and Associates but the broader involvement of the various teachers and teaching traditions, with which some of you have had contact and experience.

It is difficult to do it on your own — we are not going to say it is impossible. For example, there have been the old sages within the Taoist tradition who had such a deep connection to Nature that, in human terms, they seemed to live and grow Spiritually in isolation. In fact, they did it by aligning so closely with the powerful and illuminated life forms within the natural kingdoms, they just Ascended anyway. And if you attune to the teachings of Lao Tse, or the original thoughts of Chuang Tze, you can get an essence of that alignment.

For most of you, however, living in a Western society, undistorted nature is rare. You can gain inspiration from interacting with any form of Nature and even more from growing plants, trees and flowers etc, seeing life coming into Being before you. However it may be a simpler and more reliable Path to develop the relationships with your group and/or one-on-one with the teaching Masters of the Spiritual Hierarchy.

Questions and Answers

How long will it take in Earth time for the Earth to complete her Ascension?

We are in a process which is very hard to fit into the Gregorian calendar with which you measure time, but it would seem to be more a matter of months rather than years for the Earth to complete this process. There is not a great deal of time left (as you conceive of time) and many of you, who have woken up to this process, can feel each day the energy shifting – it is moving very fast, increasing exponentially. If you got used to the rate of increase last week, then you need to redouble your openness to growing faster next week. We are not exaggerating.

This is a time to go beyond anything which you thought possible. You are strong beings, you can be amazed at what you can actually do in this situation, particularly with our help.

It would be good if you can learn to risk "sticking your heads out a bit more", even while knowing the accumulated reactions that mainstream people carry with them. You will find that as events continue to unfold – not just the strange weather but the financial system going into more and more disintegration, you will find that people will be opening to hear a little more, particularly with regard to reconnecting with Spirit.

So give some thought to this, how you can work into your discussions and conversations with people some thoughts about some of the fundamental causes of what is going on. Perhaps mention some relevant and helpful things you and they can do so as not to feel total outcasts, or indeed alienation from the whole Ascension process. Do some homework, make some preparations, tryout talking with people who have "good hearts". Just see how much you can get across to them, without being overly too serious or sad about the whole thing. And that's quite a combination!

Why is it so important to convince other people who are deeply committed to believing the opposite. Have not people already made their choices?

In some cases there is still a possibility – we are talking about a minority. But, from the Earth's perspective, she needs there to be a number of somewhat opened Light individuals living on the surface of the new 5D Earth to build the new civilisation. She needs it and humanity's convenience is not the first priority. Yes, we are well aware that many individuals are probably unreachable at this time, but not all. You will find that children can be helped particularly.

Most adults do not talk to children very much or at all. Any adult with a cheerful heart, who can focus in and perceive what the children feel is "really going on for them" at a particular time, can establish a connection with them. And the children say "Gosh, there's an adult who actually relates to us". That is something really special. There are opportunities there.

Children are much more likely to be able to make this Ascension than their parents or other adults. Hopefully some of the children will be able to lead their parents forwards but they need some encouragement, they need a few seeds to be sown. They need to have a little reinforcement of their residual beliefs from when they came into incarnation – that there are some cheerful things and there are some positive ways of dealing with situations: love-based solutions rather than those based on fear motivation, for example.

And this is where stories can help raise the consciousness. In stories, everything is possible; that's why children love stories. And there are some adults also who have not forgotten that particular form of magic.

So however frustrating it has been talking with adults in the past, we are asking you for the next period of three months, to reach out when it seems there may be a possibility of connecting. It may or may not go anywhere but there is no judgement about that.

The results of this kind of initiative to even a very few individuals can be very beneficial for the new community of the 5D New Earth, which you are in line to be part of. We are definitely not asking for any preaching. Rather just use that subtle moment when one can work in a new understanding, a new way of looking at situations.

So we extend our blessings to each of you here in the room, each of you hearing this recording and to each of you who reads the transcript. We are available for any of you who choose to be part of this great Spiritual Enlightening, which is unfolding deeper and deeper each day.

CHAPTER FIVE
Human Evolution as your Planet Ascends

This is Quan Yin communicating from an advanced level which is not usually available for such transmissions to Spiritual groups in your world.

This is partly why the tone of our communications have a different pitch to them. Our primary goal is for the message to be eminently understandable, clear and precise. They are still very much love-based and reflect our great concern, and that of the whole Spiritual Hierarchy at this time, for humanity as you face the enormous shifts on which the Earth is already well embarked. Our concern relates to the rather thin response of individual humans facing change on a scale which is truly a revolution in your lives.

This does not mean in any way that we expect any individual to take action just because we suggest it is a good idea to do so. But, if you want to stay with this beautiful planet as she makes her transition from the OLD Earth at 3D level to the NEW Earth at 5D Consciousness, then some relevant actions are necessary.

A New Earth Stepping out of the Old

We mentioned in our previous communication that, as the 5D Earth emerges, it is almost like seeing an astral body stepping out of a physical body, although in this case the Earth's 5D "astral" body will be a little denser than the human astral body in that analogy. The special effects in your film industry would have no difficulty at all in creating a visual portrayal of this process.

The primary challenge is for humans to believe that this separation is what is already in process. From a lifetime of experience, most human individuals believe that they are very much a physical body. However, there are those of you who have studied in the Spiritual

Realms and have gradually come to understand that you are a Spirit who inhabits a physical body.

You understand that you came in as a Spirit at the beginning of your life, you follow a lifetime curriculum, you have all sorts of experiences and you exercise many choices in the course of that life. At the end, the Spirit leaves in that process often known as dying. There is of course no death involved in it, just a shift in the environment as the Spirit goes back to the Spiritual Realms.

So now we are needing to go beyond this understanding, which those of you on the Spiritual Path have worked hard to comprehend fully. We have a situation looming where a combination of the human Spiritual Body, the astral body together with a refined version of the physical body, all move on to a New World in a state of full consciousness and full functioning. Therefore it is not only the body of the Earth which steps out in a somewhat astral form to move up to a 5D level, but also humans who have aligned with the higher levels of the Earth's energies. These individuals will be able to step out and step up, so they can stay with the Earth as she Ascends.

Venus and Mars have Ascended Long Ago

This is not a particularly easy process to understand because there is no precedent for it on Earth – it's the first time it has happened with your planet. A year ago, El Morya introduced you to a highly relevant precedent in that this has happened to all the other planets in your Solar System. They have all been through this process of Ascension from the 3D level, thousands of years ago.

On Venus, it was a harmonious process during which almost all of the population, quite effortlessly, were able to step into the higher levels. But that is part of the essence of the Venus energy; they already had a good level of co-operation operating even at the 3D level.

When the message was introduced on Venus, some 100 years before the actual planetary Ascension took place, that there was a need for everybody to thoroughly work through a process of deeply under-standing this transition, they immediately set out to do so. There was not the questioning and doubting: "Well, I don't understand that" or " I don't think that's really what I want to do" and all the other reasons that people on Earth come up with as to why they do not want to grow Spiritually.

So after some 100 years very roughly in Earth time, Venus Ascended and almost 100% of the Venusian population Ascended with her. In her prior 3D state, Venus was like the current Earth in being a freewill zone and there were a very few individuals who did not want to make the transition. They preferred to stay at the 3D level and so they transferred to other planets, which had a similar 3D basis. Nobody fell through the cracks, everybody was taken care of.

That is the commitment that we make to humanity at this time. But 2012 Earth is not Venus of that pre-Ascension time. You have a much more discordant society where the "leaders", as they like to call themselves, of political, financial and social institutions are not aligned with the highest good. So that makes the challenge of these adjustments much more substantial for each of you on Earth.

You are having to do a balancing act of keeping the 3D and 4D level of activity functioning within your current lives, whether that is a business or service, while at the same time opening yourselves to a radical upgrade. This is quite a balancing act between two worlds – one fading out and one coming into being – and we want to acknowledge that this is something that won't feel straightforward.

On Mars, where the Ascension to the 5D level also happened some thousands of years ago, it was not as smooth a transition as happened on Venus. Martian energy is different – your astrological symbology contains part of the truth of the essence of Mars compared with Venus. There is a lot more to it than your astrologers talk about, but there is truth within the comparison. So as Mars ascended, about 60% of the population chose and managed to make the ascent also. The conse-quences of less co-operation and more conflict certainly took their toll.

The importance of Mars, in terms of understanding this whole process, is that it is the planet which the Earth's scientific establishment has explored most fully by various probes. The analysis and explanations that they have put forward as to what actually existed on Mars range from "they have found traces of an old civilisation", through "maybe there was water on the surface at one time" to "there's certainly nobody living there now". From our perspective, this is the "hulk" which stays at a 3D level; a residue left after the 5D part of the planet and its 5D-capable inhabitants have stepped upwards.

So there is a 5D Mars sitting side by side with the 3D hulk. However, if you're just looking at this from a 3D perspective as an observer or researcher, then you will not perceive the 5D Mars, unless personally you are already of that same level or higher. And, as harsh as it may seem to you on the Earth at this present time, this is the path with which our beautiful planet Earth is well underway, of creating a separate 5D New Earth. The good news is that the beauty, positiveness, love-based activities and the best part of Nature are all transferable to the 5D level.

The negativity and misuse of resources will all stay with the Earth's residue, once the Spirit of the Earth has moved on and upwards. But it is perhaps a consolation to know that none of the beauty on this Earth that you know and value is going to be lost for those individuals who make the Ascension also.

The Original Proposal for Physical Communities

Living on 3D Earth, it is in the nature of a positive and creative human individual to seek to build structures in terms of buildings, properties, enterprises, services and communication networks which can expand and grow. It has been normal to take a long-term view of how your way of living and your enterprise, whatever it is, can grow each year, or indeed each decade, to new heights as you explore and introduce new facets, which link together with the original foundation of your lives and your initiatives.

So we come back to the balancing act, in this interim period you need, obviously, to keep your existing work and way of living functioning — as long as there is something to function with – in terms of financial and resource distribution systems. The reason why we strongly advocated the formation of self-sufficient communities was that it would have been a much more harmonious way of making the transition. A group of aligned people coming together in a community would have found that, working with the Spiritual Hierarchy, they could have raised their energy at a much faster rate than was possible as separate individuals. More of a 24/7 experience as those of you who have lived in community know well.

This was our proposal for humanity – that, by living in such communities, a whole group could ascend without even realising that they were doing so. One day would follow another and the Ascension process would be just built-in. For an assortment of reasons we have not got into that situation, at least not in the way envisaged.

At this point, we have decided to refocus what we are offering so that it can be utilised effectively by individuals and households. We have made a commitment that it still will work – that you can still make this Ascension in this other framework.

One of the main differences between operating as individuals (or individuals within a household) compared with living in a Spiritual Community is that it becomes of much greater importance that you make a clear choice that you want to be part of the current Ascension process. You need to communicate if you want to stay with Gaia, this great Earth Spirit, as she makes her Ascension, which is well underway at this point.

The 3D Curriculum on Earth

Already in some parts of the world there are substantial Earth movements, plates shifting and hundreds of thousands of people have already been affected – it has certainly not been easy for them. It is our intention to make the process as workable as possible — humane

47

in the specific sense of not being abrasive or unnecessarily difficult, to recognise the need, so far as it is possible, to create a warm and loving experience of Ascension. Since we are deeply involved in formulating the plan for Earth's Ascension, we have the responsibility to speak from that level.

From our perspective, we have reached this decision point of whether or not you have the feeling within you to say "Yes, I'd like to be part of the New Earth and I'd like to bring with me the very best of what I've experienced on Earth so far, I'd like to bring the very best of what I've been able to create at different times, to bring all that forward". We look at the 3D Earth as a kind of training ground, perhaps a kindergarten but obviously it is not just for children. But it is a time when you have time and space to put energy into developing parts of yourselves which are more aligned with the higher levels of existence. The meditations and teaching programmes, the higher alignment with Nature and Nature Spirits, help us to understand that we are part of a great community of living beings upon the Earth, which goes far beyond just humanity.

At this 3D level, things do not all happen at once, so you have the opportunity to focus, the opportunity to try first one way and then perhaps an alternative – beginning to embrace the creative process as a normal way of living your lives. Recognising that, if you wish to grow continuously, you must be willing to release things from the past that are no longer needed. There are always quite a lot of those, from our own observations!

You have to be willing to go beyond the confines of your excellent subconscious minds, which recall everything from the past, a very useful function they were designed to do. Unfortunately, in mainstream society on Earth, for many, many individuals, the subconscious minds dutifully re-create everything from the past and so create whatever happens next, in line with what has already happened.

The process of growing Spiritually and individually requires that you have to take on the role of Spiritual Director of your lives. You listen to what your subconscious mind has to say – this chattering voice as you all experience it, the one which often won't shut up even when you ask it to, it always has its say. You have to develop a Spiritual Personality, call it "Director" or not, which can say to your subconscious mind "Thank you for that input, now this is what we are going to do in this situation".

This is a major change away from the automatic behaviour, the automatic reactions through which so many humans currently experience life, making them so easy to programme by the political and commercial groups that wish to control how people think. If you are geared up to relating to what you have done or experienced in the past, then you are very easy to control. As you go further and further into the Spiritual Path and you choose to go beyond what you have done previously, you achieve a measure of freedom and some independence from the groups within society which want you to do what they want.

This is not rocket science but it is not understood by much of humanity. Some of the processes within Spiritual workshops and meditation training have an essence of beginning to face up to this. In this poignant challenge which you are facing now, it does help to recognise explicitly that its OK to release a lot of what you believed life was about. As you go through this huge transition, if you so choose, you have to be willing to let go some of the "old stuff" which is no longer needed or appropriate, including aspects on a physical level.

This is not a particularly popular message because the most comfortable approach to life is to just keep on pretty much as you have done in the past. You just make a few changes here or there to keep the energy flowing and produce a little liveliness in what you're doing.

Becoming Part of Gaia's New Earth

At this time the Earth, your "hostess" in the very specific sense that she is the planetary body on whose surface you live, is making changes which are not in small increments. If you want to keep up with her, you are going to need to be willing to go far beyond what has seemed possible and comfortable in the past.

In some ways, as Gaia has delayed, perhaps almost to the last moment for her actual Ascension to the 5D level, it has become a bit of a rush instead of the orderly process we described taking place on Venus, where training and experiential work was carried out over an extended period, enabling most people to move forward steadily.

Gaia has been very busy creating the extraordinary level of beauty on Earth, but she came round to the understanding that it was very important that she Ascended, not just for all those lifeforms in and on her planetary body, but also for the whole Solar System and indeed within our Galaxy. She is learning fast and she is committed.

We in the Spiritual Hierarchy are doing our level best to get this message out to humanity or specifically those parts of humanity that have a reasonable likelihood of choosing to stay with the Earth as she goes up. For those of you who are clear about this goal and wish to move forward, you do not have to go through difficult examinations or have special skills, it is a process of having an open Heart Centre, a love-based approach to living life and to have worked out most of your accumulated karma through being of service.

Then you say "Yes, I want to be part of the Ascension, I want to be part of the New Earth". If you can be excited about it, that is even better – it helps others to join in! We will do the rest from that point onwards, you will receive more and more communications coming directly from us, coming through your heart and your crown. You will certainly not be left to work this out on your own.

But we realise it is not for everybody. The experience you have had at the 3D level is of tremendous value. Some people may want to have work opportunities, have more living at that 3D level and there is nothing wrong with that – you just have to change planets to carry on.

Our Commitment to each Individual's Safe Evolution

As we said before, nobody is going to be allowed to slip through the cracks, everybody will be held and contained – we will make sure of this – this is the commitment of the entire team of the Spiritual Hierarchy and the Divine Feminine. Every individual will be guided to the place they need to be in next; in terms of what decisions they have made either to stay with the Earth as she Ascends, or not to stay with the Earth.

In some ways, given the state of governments and societies on Earth at the present time, it is quite understandable that many individuals expect chaos. That is what the current "controllers" (we prefer that word to "leaders") are experts at creating as the result of their actions and inactions, their devious agendas etc. It's all part of the 3D experience, having this contrast between positive and negative.

There is not going to be a role for that at the 5D level, where co-operation and an outstanding level of a universal exchange of love are the standard. All individuals and all species recognise the livingness in all things – that is an enormous difference.

When you have been experiencing life at this 3D level on Earth, it is hard to trust any organisations and institutions down here nowadays. It seems that everything they touch goes wrong almost immediately or you find out that they were not telling the truth. So a level of disbelief tends to take hold within any individual living through this current time, a disbelief that any mainstream group, any organisation can possibly arrange anything for the positive benefit of others – even though in the past there have been some outstanding charitable institutions (some foundations of the Quakers come to mind) who did succeed in a real process of giving to people in need, at least for a while.

So we want to reassure you that, when we say we will take care of every individual whether or not they choose to make this Ascent, this is not an empty promise or a forecast. We have thought this through in great detail from the higher levels of consciousness.

We understand that these levels may seem a little out of reach, while you're incarnated on Earth in a very mixed 3D level. But at our levels the projections are made, the new reality is formed and we follow through on it. We co-operate and are intimately linked with all the other great beings within the Spiritual Hierarchy, whether they be Ascended Masters, within the Realms of Archangels or Great Beings at levels above any of these.

As we work together, energies are formed of great strength, new worlds come into being according to our Spiritual Design, so we offer this assurance to you: that this one is working. It is not at this stage dependent on anything humanity collectively chooses; the choice is for the individual to join in or not. In some ways, the very highest level of choice is when an individual looks at and considers two broad directions in which they could move forwards and says from the heart: "This is the next Path for me".

So this is what we are asking you to do. There's no right or wrong of any sort. The way the choice is structured, you choose YES to go with the Ascension process or not. An absence of choice is the same as choosing "no" – this keeps it simple. Sitting on the fence is not an option if you want to Ascend.

CHAPTER SIX
Ascension Questions and Answers

What is the time frame for the Ascension?

Unfortunately, the process of Ascension does not fit the Gregorian Calendar. As the consciousness of the planet moves upwards, it is more like the tuning signal on a radio set changing as the frequencies rise but there is no correspondence with particular days, weeks and months within this year. This vast shift is something in the "now": it is not something for next week or the week after or "see how we feel in a few months time".

When you know that you've got 6 or 9 months available, there's a tendency to put the whole thing off until quite near the end of this period and decide at the last minute to act or not. What we are explaining is that you are already at that point when its going to happen tomorrow – not necessarily literally but in terms of the critical need for taking action to prepare. It is not that you have to turn your whole 3D world upside down, it is more about going within yourself and see which direction you want to go.

You are all warmly invited to sign on to this joyful journey, if you have not already done so. But it is rather like catching or missing a train: if the train has left without you, you can have all the regrets you want or you can just accept that you did not really want to be on the train, which is fine. But there is very little "wiggle room" left on this one. So we are just speaking very plainly to that effect.

Will the transition occur all at the same time?

It is already occurring in stages. The Earth is a huge multi-dimensional enterprise in terms of many different aspects of her "livingness", so she has to move some parts of herself up before others. She has been moving up very steadily now for a period and it's like an exponential growth. She is really moving very strongly forward. So there is no time left to "hum and hah" about all this.

Could you describe what is going to happen to us in the transition?

The subjective experience will vary – maybe quite a lot – between individuals who are at different stages, with different states of mind, body and emotion. Individuals who are very, very clear, who have an open Heart Centre and a tremendous heart orientation in relating to life, in many ways they will just wake up each day and the energy will have moved them onwards – the trees will look greener, the flowers will smell with greater fragrance, people will become warmer and more joyful around them and the process continues to open up.

There will be Spiritual work which happens during the dream time (when and where we work with those who have expressed the wish to sign on) to help these committed individuals raise their energies by giving them appropriate experiences during the dreams, opening them up to being part of a huge community at this 5D level, instead of the more modest number of people you are used to interacting with. Then, at a certain point, you won't come back from the dream but you are still in the dream. That is how that kind of individual might experience it.

We are not saying that is how it's going to be for everybody. There are substantial differences in personal readiness. For individuals for whom it's more of a stretch, it is likely to be more of a bumpy ride. They may suddenly find that parts of their lives, which they believed to be part of themselves, may suddenly drop away. This might feel surprising, hopefully not shocking, but certainly surprising. Please be aware, for those of you who have signed on to this process, part of our process of conditioning is having you feel OK about change, radical change, whether or not you experience that.

The more work you have done on yourselves up to now, the more seamless your ascent will be. But for those individuals who tend to put everything off to the last minute, rather like the Earth has done herself, then it may be a much bumpier ride. However, it won't be fatal and we will be looking after you. We have provided a safety net but, as anybody who has been a circus acrobat or tightrope walker might relate, it is not a happy situation to fall into a safety net, rather than getting to the point they are aiming at. But it's definitely better than falling on the ground.

So we offer this in clarification that, however bumpy it may seem, we are not going to let you fall, once you have said this is the direction you want to go. This is our way of expressing community, by making an absolute commitment to those individuals willing to make their commitment to the overall project.

The outcome experienced is likely to be somewhere between the "seamless beautiful journey" and a "very bumpy ride". Whereabouts in that range it is for you depends on what you have done up to now, what you do henceforth and how open you are to finding this path within you. Individuality is something to be celebrated – your expression of life has got you to be at his time and place; it is from where we will help you to move forwards. So you have a range of possibilities.

Can you tell us how the three books (The Revolution of 2012) written by Andrew correspond to what we are being told now?

Well, the books were written by Catherine, while Andrew was the scribe and, to some extent, the editor, although we had views about the editing also.

The reason the books were written in three volumes was because the situation and the energy was changing quite rapidly over the period 2001 to 2009 Gregorian time. Situations and perspectives shifted during that time period, not always for the better. There was the great hope that the community projects would really take hold and people would realise that this was a great way to move forward and grow. We totally recognise and respect that community was not what most people wanted to do, except for a few gallant pioneers.

So had the communities come into being, they would have enabled our energy to be focused in much more intensely. More and more the individuals making up such self-sufficient communities would not have had to interface with the outside world to the same extent as if you are living in a private household. So the energy environment could be raised continually and consistently. This was going to be the most painless way of making the Ascension.

Although the structure of the three books in the Revolution of 2012 series is as valid now as it was when it was written down, the context has somewhat moved on. The actual description of the 5D societies has not changed at all. The consciousness of the readers, however, has risen so that the communications that we have been putting through during the last four months, from ourselves and El Morya, are pitched at a much higher level than was possible with the books in the period up to April 2009. The books are aimed at a much wider audience. What you are hearing in these recent transmissions is aimed for a much smaller number of individuals, who are already quite close to deciding to sign on to the Ascension programme.

Much of what was advocated for the forming of the physical communities is still applicable for bringing virtual communities into being. Within these, individuals who understand the process that is going on, spend a lot of time living together, having joint activities, maintaining communications, sharing what is going on in their lives and forming a very deep friendship at the very least. In these ways, you are getting some of the social benefits of community and we can also focus our energy on you with greater effect.

We are aware that some of the people who are being drawn towards being in community are not necessarily very interested in wanting to know much or indeed anything about the Ascension process. So we have a slight difference emerging here between the current communication and particularly Vol.3 of The Revolution of 2012 series.

Had the physical communities got going, then those individuals, who at the moment perhaps are not so interested in the Ascension context, would have just been drawn into the Spiritual involvement, as the focused energies just got stronger and stronger. But because you're living separately and you get together every 2/3 weeks and not everyone can come on a particular date, it is much more difficult to create that consistency, even with the best of efforts.

The basic concept of Vol. 2 – of the splitting of the dimensions – has not changed at all from the way it was described. But within that, the shift of focus from physical community to virtual community is probably the biggest change of the last six months.

Is there anything we can do as individuals to show that we are wanting to Ascend?

The very best thing to do is affirm your intention every morning in your meditation. If you call on us by name Quan Yin you will dutifully be registered and taken on board. Quite a simple process, although being in the 3D level Earth, as soon as any individual decides to "sign on" you will probably be confronted with various sorts of challenge and opposition from the darker side of all livingness here on Earth. What's New! Just persevere anyway.

It is just a matter of re-affirming everyday that you want to be part of the Ascension – maybe allowing yourself to dream a little. You can use your imagination and envisage all the living things on the Earth at present that you like and value moving up and being part of the New Earth. Use all your imagination to see what you can bring forward for the New Earth – what you would love to contribute. Get into the creation process. By making the daily affirmation and connection, we will stay in touch with you continuously. If you want, you can ask Andrew what this is like. But the connection is very real if you want it.

Once the Ascension process is completed, there is a process of integration into a new kind of society, a much smaller one. There will be Light Beings coming over from more evolved planets like Venus and Mars. They will bring their experience of creating these higher level societies, which are effectively of a multi-planetary nature. You certainly would not want to be re-inventing the equivalent of the wheel at this 5D level. But there will also be a great sharing in a very loving way. Although there will be quite a lot of work to do, at the 5D level you don't have to work all the time – there is always time to do lots of joyful things, even when you're founding a New Earth.

Where does the Fifth Dimension exist?

The question "Where?", is somewhat linked to the concept of the three dimensions of length, breadth and height. The Fifth Dimension does not have a physical reference point which can be described in a physical way, which can make sense to an individual whose feet are firmly planted on 3D Earth at present. The 5D Earth sits side by side with the 3D Earth, just the same as the two levels of Mars. At the 5D version, you can see the 3D hulk but at the 3D level you cannot see "upwards". So it's not really a physical position, it just sits in juxtaposition.

One of the examples, which Catherine gave right at the beginning of Vol.1 of The Revolution of 2012, was the description of going into a crop circle, lying down on the ground on all those flattened stalks and feeling that energy. If you do that, you can move into a space where there is absolutely no time. Although you are still sort of lying on the floor of the crop circle, your consciousness goes off to another place.

We have had a portal going deeply into the old Camelot energy, where people who entered the portal, experienced absolute timelessness and almost a sense of weightlessness. This has been used as a place of initiation also. You can also consider coming to more of our events.

So it is in these directions that you can feel inside yourself what 5D consciousness really is about, but what you cannot do is work it out mentally. It is really experiential – when you are in it, it is something you live, play and work with. If you would like to experience this energy, have a word with Andrew or someone else who is directly involved with it.

Is it like a place with no space, no time - only energy?

No, that's more like 7th or 9th Dimensional reality.

At 5D level, there are quite a number of 3D features that translate, like lighter emotions, for example. You still have a clearly identifiable body, but its much less dense. If you touch another person's hand on the 3D Earth, you feel just the sensation of "touch" itself, that is the solidness of the other person's physical body, the texture, the warmth and, with more sensitive people, you can sometimes feel a loving overtone to the touch.

If you touch somebody's hand at 5D, the energy can flow throughout the other person's body, depending on your wish to communicate deeply. You are not intruding because there are receptive levels which exist so as to be able to receive transmissions from just a touch.

Because the bodies are less dense, there is a lot more scope for a "touch in depth". It's like the actual molecules merge into each other for some moments then perhaps "unmerge" when the touch is concluded. If you apply your imagination, you can see there is a lot of scope for having very, very deep relationships between individuals, since you can have that depth of connection when you just touch them.

The other great part of it within your individual being, is that you have telepathic (wave) communication as a normal way of communicating. You go far beyond all the limitations of words. Some of you may have had a glimpse of this experience even in this world, when you were close enough and aligned enough with another person that thoughts, feelings and preferences just transferred to some extent. At 5D there is a multiple into the hundreds in terms of intensity.

At the 5D level , the telepathic communication happens automatically, moving figuratively to advanced "broadband" level, rather than basic "dial-up". And it goes on from there. Think about how in this society you exist in a state of separation, misunderstanding, lack of trust coupled with ongoing non-cooperation. Imagine what it would be like when everybody is part of an extended family and, even if you have not met an individual before, there is a whole transmission that introduces the person to you – and shows them accurately and truthfully, because it is impossible to distort or conceal the energetic transmission being made available.

It really is a New World but enough of it is recognisable that you can still feel and learn to become very much at home there. You can experience enormous fulfilment from being part of it. Another very important aspect is that you have a relationship with much higher levels of Spirit, while still being fully aware of your individuality. It's like you're living on one level and reaching up, aspirationally perhaps, to a higher level. You are present as an individual and experience life through a very large family-like community.

So what happens in the 4th Dimension – do we pass through it or are we in it now?

This is a temporary dimension as it makes much sense to pass through this transitional phase. All of you here are at the 4D level. There is, of course, a lower 4th and an upper 4th, but it's still a big step up from even the upper 4th to the 5D level. Everything that has been experienced at the 4D level is immensely valuable: learning about transition, learning about alternative ways of living and creating.

How can I be of Service?

There are many ways of being of service. There is a preparatory phase in which you develop perceptions of how people can be helped. Obviously, one does not wish to intrude. At the 5D level you won't because you just look and read the energy pattern. Currently you are in the 4D transitional phase where you are learning to discern how to be of service. It does not have to be anything dramatic.

We visited a local friend yesterday – a down to earth individual who has made some good Spiritual progress in recent times. He described how his next door neighbours had lost their son in a drowning accident. He said that it was so difficult to know what to say to them, so he took round some apples for them. He looked at what the neighbours were going through and felt it through his heart. He understood that words did not mean anything in an extreme situation like that so he found another way to connect, while expressing a loving and compassionate concern.

Now the people around you may not say what they need but, if you observe and interact with them, you will be able to sense what they would be open to receiving. So you have to perhaps develop a sense of theatre whereby you can find ways to gauge helping them meet their needs. It may help to get away from being too serious about it all. Find a simple way

With the state that your society is in, probably 80% of the population desperately needs help, whether or not they have enough clarity to even know that. With a neighbour, just taking an interest, sharing what's going on in life helps them feel less isolated – that's a real service in itself. Just knowing that somebody cares about them.

How can I get through to my Family?

You can only help them from where you are and there is nothing external which gets in the way, like values and beliefs. It is how you engage with people which determines how energy flows or does not flow. If you want to stay connected with your family (in the 2012 context), then the best way is to help them get an idea of what is going on in the world. If you see an opportunity, you subtly help them to feel that they have a positive opportunity to Ascend, in whatever manner has some meaning for them. But if they do not understand what is going on, there is not an awful lot you can do, except to love them.

The present situation on Earth is not sustainable. The changes are already happening to the Earth and this is being reflected in every institution and organisation on the surface of the Earth. Great cracks are appearing in governments, commercial and service organisa-tions. These cracks bring them to a standstill sometimes and enable shrewd external observers to see the truth about what is really going on inside them – quite a revelation in some cases. With all this in the background, the kindest thing to do with those you love is to help them move up as well. You cannot make them, but you can help them to wake up until such point they either do so or they say "I don't want to hear another word about it". Either way, you will have done your best.

At what point do you let go of your Responsibility?

You do your best and you will feel at a certain point if it has become a "lost cause".

Would it be true to say that when you make the choice yourself to Ascend that it helps others to make their own choices because you're no longer holding back?

Very much so. This is one of the keys to understanding how the concept of "Virtual Community", which we talked about earlier, can work very positively. While it may not be as effective as a physical community because it's more diluted, your committed choice can enable people to find their individual ways to "sign on" realising that "this is what I've been waiting for all my life, or indeed the last ten lifetimes"! The excitement and joyfulness of the Spiritual interaction is infectious.

So the group is a lot more effective than an individual on their own, even though they are doing their level best. As Jesus said: "When two or more are gathered in my Name, I am there among them". And when six or more are gathered in our Name, then it is an exponentially stronger presence. But for each of you as individuals, the clarity of your choice to go ahead with the Ascension, "signing on" each day, re-affirming your movement along the Golden Path (The Revolution of 2012, Vol.2), "Yes, I want to continue moving along the Golden Path to 5D Consciousness".

We are being quite informal about this for we do not want people to get caught up in religious-like structures. This is a straightforward process once you have the feeling within you. And, yes, once you have that feeling clearly within you, the more potential there is for those around you to wake up to the new realities unfolding.

How will we experience the split between those that Ascend and those that don't want to? Will we just wake up one day and people just won't be there anymore, or will there be deaths through accidents or other causes?

At the end of the process of reaching the 5D level, each person who gets there will know the truth about what they have been through. In contrast, those who have chosen (actively or passively) to stay on at the 3D level will not understand the process. For them, their attention will be with a process of re-education in their new body on a new planet, both of which will be available.

This process of separation is already happening. It becomes more and more difficult for people at the most basic levels of the mainstream to have any interaction with those on the Golden Path, unless those on the Golden Path actually want to have that connection. It is not recommended at the moment since you do not have time to waste, given the rush you are facing since Gaia has put off her Ascension to the "last minute".

You certainly do not want to get involved in activities which dissipate your energy and which do not move you and others forward on the Golden Path itself. It is not particularly comfortable when you're in the framework of family and friends – people you care about – who are just wanting to carry on living a very different kind of life.

The very finest expression on your part is to accept that they have an absolute right to choose whatever they do, after you have made some attempt to broach the fact that things are not going to continue as they have been. You do what you can to put this across. We have heard many stories about people's reaction to the suggestion that the Ascension is happening, with a great deal of denial and indignation etc. You may have experienced some of it yourselves.

The finest service you can offer to another person is to finally accept them and their reality just as they are, even if they have chosen to head in a completely different direction. That is a real expression of love and caring. But we ask each of you to do whatever you can to get the message across so that these people have some awareness that there is indeed a choice.

Do we need our physical body as we Ascend or is it like dying, this moving on to the next dimension?

The physical body just becomes less dense, rather like the astral body stepping out of the physical body, but it's slightly different with the human body, compared with the Earth's process. With the Earth, there is a physical hulk left behind at the 3D level. However, with the human individuals who Ascend, the actual cells within your body change their vibrational rate so your whole body becomes attuned at this new 5D level. The body becomes lighter and more flexible and it is from that basis that you Ascend.

The meditation practices that we have been offering for some five years now are designed to help in this process by changing the cellular structure of the body from being carbon-based to crystalline-based. In this way, every cell of the body becomes able to receive and transmit to a very high level – that's why the communication is so clear at the 5D level, compared with 3D. At 5D, you are not just communicating with your eyes, ears, speech, gestures and touch – every cell of your body communicates with every cell of the other person. It is a Quantum leap.

So we'll become like a Crystal?

Well, you'll have something in common but you will still have arms and legs and still able to move around. The life of a crystal is a bit more static in most cases.

So will we become ultra-sensitive to energies like Electricity and similar on Earth?

Yes, you have already made some progress in that direction.

How do people on different Dimensions relate?

All dimensions inter-relate with each other but the 3D and below are relatively isolated since the higher dimensions can relate to them but

3D etc cannot relate upwards. So for this time, it is best to focus on where you are now and the choice that is available to you – where you can move to. It is a highly complex situation and we have had to simplify it to make it understandable at your current level.

Once you have Ascended to 5D, there is a world with a perpetual sense of clarity, joyfulness and acceptance about which individuals, who have left their bodies and communicated back through the channelling process, have shared. That is how you will come to experience and understand it. It is very difficult to make any progress in comprehending all this using a mental approach, although we fully understand the curiosity, the wish to know and the wish to understand.

It is only through experiencing the energies that you will understand them. So find some ways, if you are interested, of experiencing the higher levels. Sitting in this room is one of them but there are quite a number of other ways, we have mentioned one or two already. We do convene meetings from time to time – we would have them more often if people wanted them – so you can feel these energies in every cell of your body and being.

In the books, we have described this as a "total immersion" process because that is the most straightforward way to understand it. It's like learning a foreign language. You could just set out with a row of books and labour away, mentally trying to figure it out and remember "what you say when". But the natural way of learning a foreign language is to just move to that country and learn to swim of necessity. In the process, you don't just learn but you feel, remember, and link all the linguistic parts to something real that's happening in life. There is quite a correlation in all this with the Ascension process.

In conclusion, we give our blessings to each of you and, as part of our love for you, we respect unconditionally the choices you make, whether to be part of the Ascension or not. You will always be loved. At the 5D level, you will feel it more.

CHAPTER SEVEN
El Morya –Maintaining a
Balance during the Last Lap

Some of you, quite naturally, have wondered how the blossoming may progress in this year of 2012, the year full of promise and expectation in terms of the Earth's Ascension to 5D. In particular, you have wondered "What is going to happen"?

Some of you have made preparations during this winter period, building on what you achieved last year. But the question continues to hang in the air: "What is going to happen and when"? You hear perhaps that the Spirit of the Earth (Gaia) is making reasonable progress in her movement along the Path of Planetary Ascension. But this does not give you a date or even a month when you can say "I know that it is going to happen then".

It would be nice in human terms, in the current values of the society in which you live, to be able to put it in your diary or calendar, saying "I'm keeping this month clear", at least. But, as we have pointed out a number of times now, the sequence of advance, the sequence of stages that the Earth must go through during her advance along her Ascension Path, do not fit in any way the characteristics of the Gregorian calendar, to which your society is strongly wedded.

Most people do not realise that this calendar is quite recent within human history. It was one of the many unfavourable innovations which came with the Roman age – it was part of their system of control, which was their main expertise. In the British Isles, it was not until 900 AD that time and calendars were standardised throughout the country. Thus a great deal of flexibility, which had been available in previous ages, just disappeared.

So the Earth's Ascension, an event which is gathering momentum and moving forward steadily, is instead regarded by humanity as something uncomfortable. It is important to realise that most of that uncomfortableness is due to your expectation of being able to slot these future events into your calendar. In saying this, we're not in any way putting down the sensible use of a calendar – it is a coping mechanism in what some people term "a crazy world".

The reason why we are drawing your attention to this interaction between two incompatible energy systems is that it is the source of these questions which are coming up all the time amongst the relatively small numbers of humans who understand enough of the process of the Earth's Ascension for it to be part of their day by day life.

A Need for a Balancing Act

In the last major discourse from Quan Yin (Chapters 5/6), she drew your attention to the nature of the balancing act which you are all being required to perform. On the one hand, you need to be open and ready for the Ascension, both planetary and your own on an individual basis. On the other hand, you need to maintain your "everyday life", where things need to be taken care of in terms of life support, serving the others in your life who need you, as well as maintaining your business or profession in a responsible manner. So what we are going to do this morning is to provide an energy rebalancing, which will help you perform this balancing act between these two endeavours.

In the animal, vegetable and plant world (including the trees), there are many lessons which one can learn, which are applicable to the human experience. One of these is patience, along with a willingness to be available – just to be "present".

When you watch a plant growing, it focuses its energy on its current functioning – allowing the life force to flow through all its fibres, with some of the energy going to the new growth. There is an awareness within many plants that their lives may be curtailed or even terminated by external events. This is built into the species' understanding and knowledge but you notice that the plant just keeps on anyway.

Although this may not be an exact analogy (as always), there is a tremendous amount to be learned from watching, from taking in the ways of functioning within Nature. This is particularly important when you're doing this balancing act between keeping your everyday life moving along, while being aware of what is a virtual certainty that the Planetary Ascension happens and 3D Earth will fade into oblivion. After that, things which humanity has been used to being provided with, will have passed on too.

So we are suggesting, on a daily basis, in addition to affirming that you wish to be part of the process, that you are moving along the Golden Path to your individual Ascension to higher levels, that you also visualise a healthy growing plant that is yourself – you just choose the plant that you like the best. And like the plant, you continue to grow right through this period of "not knowing when the big one is going to happen", so to speak.

In this context, the "big one" does not refer to the actual external events; rather it is the time to make your major individual Ascension. This will coincide with when the 5D version of the Earth pulls away from the old 3D residue, as already clearly described (Chapters 5/6). But the real focus is not on the external event happening. Rather your focus needs to be on being ready yourself – on being this vibrant plant, ready for whatever comes. As you observe Nature, that is how they are. Even though you may know that they are going to be harvested the next day, the corn or wheat growing in the field continues to grow up to the very last moment.

The Artist's Approach to Individual Ascension

Fortunately, you are not facing that rather dramatic form of harvesting, but the same principles apply. See yourself in vibrancy each morning – "How can I grow more fully this day, how can I help others grow"? Focus on the present, being in each of those successive moments which go to make up the day. If you find yourself going into nostalgia, looking backwards, wishing things could have been different, comparing things continually with the past, as most have done sometimes – please realise it does not lead anywhere in this particular context.

This appropriate way of looking at the day has sometimes been compared with the outlook of an artist, who starts the day with a blank canvass. They begin to create that day, putting in some outlines, shapes and structures – then filling in, putting some "flesh on the bones", as their graphic illustration expands. But what they do not do is include the future or the past; this picture/this day exists as an entity in its own right.

Now of course everything that you have been through in the past is indeed what has brought you to the point where you can be at that moment of creation of the new day. What we are bringing forward is that this new day really is NEW, after living through all the previous days, months, years and indeed lifetimes. You are at this point – you are the creator, the artist.

There is an old saying from the 1960s "She's an artist, she don't look back". This is a piece of profound wisdom which fits our concepts well. The rationale follows that everything that you do within your day is because you are a Spiritual creator – you are alive in this minute and you are alive in the next moment. You do not need a mental justification for being alive for it is a Spiritual process, a Spiritual flow.

Of course, your mind is going to have its commentary on "what's going on". The subconscious mind has been described in this way in the teachings of the Brotherhood, over and over again. It is vital to understand the freedom within this creation process of each day – it is the path to your individual freedom. Even when you are surrounded by all the constraints seemingly imposed by outside forces: other people, institutions, organisations or whatever, you can still exercise this freedom.

Your job in expressing this lifeforce at its strongest is to be that beautiful plant which just keeps on growing each day. Yet each day is always unique in the way that you or the plant grow. We suggest and strongly recommend that you bring your whole consciousness much, much closer to being in the present time, as an ongoing practice.

CHAPTER EIGHT
The Purpose of the
Fifth Dimensional Network

At certain times in the history of humanity, there has been a direct intervention from the high Spiritual Realms to ensure that a certain transition could take place. These were particularly geared towards those individuals who volunteered to be part of the planned journey of change and evolution to a new plane or, indeed, to a new world.

Such acts of creative intercession have sometimes occurred near the end of a cataclysmic cycle, when an old order has become sufficiently corrupted and confused that societies could no longer evolve. These time periods have often been associated with environmental pollution and overpopulation to an extent that constrained the Earth's very ability to breathe and were therefore unsustainable.

There have also been other initiatives not related to the necessary arrangements pertaining to the end of a cataclysmic cycle which focused instead on the creation of a new world of Love and Light. This was to enable individual humans, who had fulfilled their curriculum of evolution and growth, to step directly into a new arena of life experience and, so to speak, "hit the ground running", without having to go through the usual death and reincarnation processes.

The Implementation of the Fifth Dimensional Network

At this time of late Spring 2012, we have in mind both these precedents of functional purpose as we move forwards with the implementation of our Fifth Dimensional Network (Dnet for short). This is an organisational and energetic structure to enable those members of humanity, who choose to evolve to the Fifth Dimensional (5D) New Earth, to make the journey in relative safety and comfort, notwithstanding a background of increasing chaos and destruction.

We have specifically designed the Dnet to fulfil three design criteria: to provide absolute protection from lower frequency entities of all kinds, to provide a continual flow of enlightened energy to each participant and a direct connection to the Fifth Dimensional Source to enable a fundamental inner adjustment to the energies of the New Earth. Unless an individual chooses to leave the Dnet (that choice is available at any time), there will be an automatic and continual Ascension to whatever level of 5D is attainable for them in the time and space available before the Earth completes her own Ascension.

The design of the sphere surrounding each participant follows energetic patterns of protection which have been used for many thousands of years. We know it works well – this is very far from being an "untried technology".

The Great Wisdom in the Central Sphere

The protection provided is not in any way at the expense of the ability to communicate. The infrastructure of tubes and shafts joining individuals' spheres to the Central Sphere allows a great bandwidth of positive and light energy to flow. The great Wisdom of the Spiritual Masters and Archangels focused in the Central Sphere is continually available to be absorbed 24/7 – in manageable doses by each participating individual within their spheres. In addition, the tubes and shafts can be installed to join together individuals' spheres so that a close family, a group of friends or even a Spiritual Community can help each other grow consistently through the exchange of positive Light energy.

The connection to the 5D energy of the New Earth through the Dnet enables each participant, within their individual sphere, to attune to the very different energies, balances and values in a steady, continual flow of love and understanding. The protection built into the network ensures that there is no distortion possible.

The Transition to 5D

When the Earth finally enters the 5D realms of consciousness, the whole of the Dnet will find themselves transferring also. From that point onwards, the protection aspect becomes of secondary importance, but the connections to the Central Sphere and the 5D Energy will remain open and available for as long as necessary. This will enable even the slowest of evolving students to complete their work of adjustment to the New World in which they find themselves.

This is the fulfilment of my promise made in Chapters Five and Six that any individual choosing to invoke my name in "Signing On" each morning to join and then move along the Golden Path to Fifth Dimensional Consciousness will in fact be taken there.

Given the now very short time remaining before life as a traditional incarnated human becomes a high-risk option, we have ensured that our new Dnet creation is very straightforward to join and live joyfully within, provided there is a sincere heart-felt desire for each individual wishing to be part of the New Earth. That means giving the development of this new alignment priority over the myriad of non-essential distractions and diversions into which even those humans on the Spiritual Path sometimes choose to put their attention and energy.

PART TWO:

THE FIFTH DIMENSIONAL
NETWORK (Dnet)

CHAPTER NINE
El Morya - The Transition to
the 5D New Earth using the Dnet

Some people have gradually become aware over the last ten years or so that they, and the rest of humanity, are on the brink of some quite new development in how life on Earth is unfolding. Their inner senses become conscious of this evolutionary change getting under way, without having a clear understanding of the outcome. A few have perceived the pattern of small incremental changes near the beginning of the pattern but rising to a peak of exponential change as we approached the vicinity of the Winter Solstice 2012.

While we in the Spiritual Hierarchy have endeavoured to get out some understanding of these evolutionary processes, albeit with somewhat mixed results, within human activities it was, all too often, the soft option version of the Earth's evolution which was presented in the various "New Age" workshops, books and articles. In this misleading scenario, an individual would just evolve perfectly, even though they did little or nothing to make changes for the better in their individual lives.

Life is What You Make of It

For our part, we attempted to emphasise the truth that some wiser individuals have learned to understand, while still living in the third dimensional (3D) realms — that life is what you make of it. Your life is what you speak, the energies you project, the actions you take and whether your orientation to others is of a loving and supportive kind, or not so much. As each person progresses along their Life Destiny Path, the choices they make, what they say or do, how much of a loving attitude they bring to each moment of the day — all these determine the outcomes within the karmic possibilities and probabilities of each individual's Life Destiny Path.

This is why the skill and wisdom of the Guidance of the Higher Self is so important in designing each individual soul's Life Destiny Pattern. When it has been well chosen, an individual apparently just living a quite ordinary life can reach extraordinary levels of Consciousness within themselves through using certain techniques and understandings, notwithstanding all the choices and possibilities.

The workings of the cause/effect patterns are equally true and apparent when it comes to the momentous event of the Earth's Ascension. It is what you choose that is relevant to this unprecedented situation that determines your personal outcome. What each individual needs is a full opening at deep inner levels to enable them to cope with the new refined vibrations of the 5D New Earth.

Helping Gaia with her Ascension

In aggregate, the opening up of even some individuals directly affects and augments Gaia's ability to make her Ascension, so there is some co-creation taking place. Sometimes Gaia's strong endeavours to raise herself up to the 5D level bring back images of ancient times when Hercules was holding up the whole world – a tremendous weight on his shoulders. This is part of the feeling Gaia has at present — with so many people oblivious of what she needs from them at this time to help her make her move upwards.

Even within the mainstream, it is of considerable value to Gaia's process when people join together in any group of genuine goodwill, where people are treated with warmth and respect on a consistent basis. This creates a benevolent energy which Gaia can use in forging her way upwards. The more people come together in groups, where they can be positive, light hearted and joyful, the more this lightens the burden on your great planetary Spirit Gaia.

Conversely, when individuals of negative intent create war, deception, financial collapse and other destructive outcomes, Gaia's upward movement is constrained and obstructed. Because negative events are reported so fully in the media, their effect is reinforced by so many people's belief that these situations are inevitable and even "normal". Hence there is much need to balance this negativity with energies of warmth, light, beauty and positiveness.

However, there is an enormous need for some people, at least, to go beyond just a joyful expression of life, useful though that is in aggregate. We need some individuals, who are willing and motivated, to open up from within and connect at a deeper level with the profound understandings of what life on Earth is really about. They need to be willing to make the inner transition to learning to control and centre their subconscious mind, so it does not operate continually as the basis for current decisions.

Ideally, the subconscious mind becomes an obedient servant, listening to what we call the "Spiritual Director" of their life, going beyond the mental/emotional internal chatter, commentary and reaction, which the mainstream believes is a normal way to live one's life on Earth. So the challenge is to look at each moment from a reflective and intuitive standpoint – before one communicates or takes action.

Creation of the Fifth Dimensional Network to Access Ancient Wisdoms

For these and many other reasons, our team from the Spiritual Hierarchy have created the Fifth Dimensional Network (Dnet). We have listened and observed carefully to what has happened in the last several thousand years. We have looked particularly at what has happened to all the many attempts and enterprises to bring Spiritual enlightenment into the forefront of living on this Earth, rather than just something that people do in a backroom.

For long periods in the history of the world, the only safe way to get together for a Spiritual group was indeed hidden away in a back room, where the forces of reaction were powerless to affect their outcomes. Because of this need for secrecy and isolation, the teaching of Spiritual knowledge, the Ancient Wisdoms, became quite piecemeal. Brave individuals, here and there, persevered to bring a deeper perspective to those seeking Spiritual Truth.

What humanity needs now is a much more general appreciation of the Spiritual Realms: the different levels of energy, the importance of the Heart Centre, the relationship with the Higher Self, the relationship of the Angelic realms with the Earth — all these elements linked together. You need to understand Guidance and how a higher level Guide functions. How do you know if you get a feeling to do something that it is coming from a high and wise place of origin or, alternatively, from a source of negative disinformation?

In the very short time remaining before the Earth completes her Ascent, we had to find a way whereby relatively large numbers of people can be exposed to the Great Wisdoms, to this great Light energy, these high vibrations — then go on to absorb and retain them. As we have taught many times, given the current state of most human minds, it is very difficult for individuals to even hear the message, let alone understand it. Yet that is crucial for any person seeking to bring this wisdom into the Heart Centre and integrate it within your whole being.

In times past, those individuals, whom had reached that sufficient opening of the Heart Centre, had taken years or decades of training and practice. They had gone through a wide variety of experiences of learning what worked and what did not, what was real and what was false.

At the present time, we have had to find a significant way for those individuals, who volunteered and really wanted to be part of the 5D New Earth, to "sign on" daily, in response to Quan Yin's very clear offer mentioned in Chapters Five and Six. They need to know that they will be taken through to be part of the new Golden Age of the 5D New Earth. This is very much part of the ethos and design of the Dnet.

We had to find a way that the Ancient Wisdoms could be absorbed by a process of Spiritual osmosis by those who had reached a certain level of perception, so they could finally graduate from the 3D curriculum. And the Dnet energy structure was what we came up with.

Within the Dnet procedures, as you tune in to form your individual sphere (Chapter Eleven) and then going on to connect with the Central Sphere, you are becoming part of an energy structure in which the Ancient Wisdoms flow to your individual sphere and the enlightening human within it. This energy flows each moment of the day and night. We designed it so that the energy flow is carefully modulated to the precise needs and capability of each Dnet individual, to enable it to be assimilated in a balanced way in every moment.

Raising your Personal Energy to the 5D Level

Within the time span available, each of you can raise your personal vibration and consciousness up to or near the level required for the 5D New Earth. Additionally, we have designed the Dnet energy structure so that each individual "signing on" and creating their own individual sphere, is completely protected at all times from any efforts of the darker elements operating in this 3D Earth, to obstruct or detach an individual from moving along this vital path towards the Light.

In many Spiritual schools in past times, which were not totally contained within a closed community with a correct orientation towards the Light, many individuals fell by the wayside, overwhelmed by the distractions, diversions and other undermining activities from the less than positive forces on 3D Earth. So we have designed the Dnet, with its twice-daily clearance and energy input, so none of the above take hold, provided an individual joins and stays connected within the Dnet.

In making this very open offer that each individual who decides to sign on to this programme will be taken up as the Earth makes her Ascent, we are aware that individuals arriving at the 5D New Earth will be in quite a variety of different states of awareness. The one thing they will have in common is an open Heart Centre and a sense of loving

81

engagement with life and all they encounter. They will be open to all kinds of new experiences in their new location.

At this point, the main priority is to allow all those individuals, who want to be part of this New World, an energy magnetism which facilitates their transfer from the old 3D Earth to the 5D New Earth, for that is what is possible in the time remaining. Because of the energetic processing within the Dnet, your body will be capable of adjusting to the much lower density of the 5D New Earth. This is another reason why joining the Dnet and being exposed to this conditioning energy 24/7 is so important.

Each of you using the Dnet will find the adjustment physically quite gentle, taking a few weeks or months to adjust to the new environment. The whole transition becomes feasible. You will be able to keep your current systems of breathing and digestion functioning in a different way. 5D residents do not eat much – they just have highly nutritious drinks for their main nourishment, but they do eat solid food occasionally.

Transitional Training Schools of the 5D New Earth

We have made provision on the 5D New Earth that there will be a series of training schools to allow each person the time, space and energy to reach a sound state of balance and understanding, from which to step into the many opportunities and novel situations available in that New World. This is how we intend to create a world of harmony, notwithstanding the diversity of the humans who made it through the many obstacles which had been put in their paths at different times. This will enable a balancing of the somewhat different prior levels achieved by the incoming humans.

In a transition place, it is quite OK for an individual to start with a quite different initial awareness, for there is sufficient time and space to fill in any gaps of understanding. This enables them to take their place in the full strength version of the 5D New Earth. It is manageable if someone is only at Dimension 4 ¾ on first arrival because we have set up the safety net and the system of retraining to cope with that. There will not be any sense of good or bad, let alone "They should have done better". There will be no judgements about what prior level you have reached.

The 5D New Earth is already well-populated with a variety of inhabitants. Some, like Catherine (the Spiritual author of The Revolution of 2012) have deliberately taken on their 5D body so they can be part of a functioning core population. This is much smaller than on the current 3D Earth. There are and will be some very beautiful beings from other planets within your Solar System, mostly from Venus and Mars but some from Jupiter and others. To help fit in, they will take on some shapes that will be more similar to the humans you are used to, at least initially.

Living with 5D Energy in the New Earth Environment

So there is a basic infrastructure in place along with a core population who are "at ease" with the new ways of living and operating at the 5D level. They have some simple buildings not unlike those you can see in some art galleries of a classical portrayal of Greek temples, usually with beautiful sunlight pouring in over the romantic Mediterranean waters.

Some of these pictures provide quite a good illustration of what it feels like to be in this beautiful Light energy. The seemingly eternal sunlight is not an exaggeration, for the higher-level Devas, who are organising this 5D New Earth, are highly skilled in balancing the humidity so that the plants have what they need without strong winds and heavy rain, let alone snow and ice. These are all worthwhile experiences to have at the 3D level but we are talking about graduating to a world with a substantially different curriculum, including the climate.

Within this gentle, warm and balmy climate, people still have their own modest size homes as private retreat space, where they create whatever energy they choose. One of the crucial differences is in the form of manifestation, which is why the initial training schools are

83

needed. You learn the ability to transmit "Wave Energy" packed with meaning, content and power – with elements of what is to be created within these "Waves".

So if you want to make your home beautiful in a different way, you create a concept within your visualisation then project the "Wave Energy" from your Heart Centre. You carry out the work with some physical action in that much less dense world, where matter responds more directly to incoming energy. Much of the creation within a home or within a community choosing to live together, is about harmonising the aspirations of those participating individuals into a joint creation, a joint focus – maybe something equivalent to beautiful music and dance.

Another community might want to concentrate on working with plants and small creatures, another might wish to work with energy systems. Maybe you have heard of the community energy systems we used in the Golden Age of Atlantis, where there was a transmission from a central tower which was picked up by each community or residential unit. It was in a perfect wave form and could quickly be adapted for any purpose within the household or community group. There is indeed a whole world of evolution should you choose to work with those energies. And there are many other ways of engaging with your prime interests.

The idea is that individuals are drawn together with those others who have similar intents. There is not the kind of "lottery" approach common in the urban environment on 3D Earth, where first you find a place to live and then find out whose living next door – with whom, as you know, you can have all sorts of mixed experiences including occasionally a positive one. It's mostly a situation of making the best of what's presented with elements of survival, neutrality and sometimes karmic culmination. On the 5D New Earth, there is a different curriculum. You deal with how far you can move forwards on a creative Path but in a co-operative way, rather than a competitive one.

Schedule for Moving to 5D

It is certainly not a simultaneous event – quite different from the fundamentalist Christian concept of "The Rapture" where, in a great flash of light, all the church members elevate.

As the weeks pass, you will find that the energy of the Dnet becomes more and more distinct. In terms of the personal balancing act between keeping your 3D life functioning and what you are experiencing in getting more and more into the 5D level, the latter will just become stronger and stronger – and individual after individual will transfer into this cascade of Light.

There will be some within the Network who will go first and will have a role to play as an "advance party", preparing the core group already settling the 5D New Earth. They will advise what it's going to be like having this bunch of humans arriving in all different states of consciousness. You can envisage that there is a major briefing exercise to be undertaken. For their part, the core group will be able to learn from teaching and debriefing this advance party what they need to know – observing how effective different teaching methods are going to be.

There is a major learning process going on so, by the time the mass of the Dnet participants arrive, they will have got themselves organised and prepared to cater for however many categories are needed, in the various fields of endeavour, to make things fit. There will be inevitably be the last persons to make the transfer being at Dimension 4 ½ or 4.6, or whatever it is, for them it will be a big stretch. While it is not out of reach, it is hard work and they are going to need the most help in making the final step.

We have no doubt that these latecomers will make it through, since we designed an appropriate safety net but, as Quan Yin put it, they may end up having a bumpy ride. In the process, they will be able to work off more of the last residues of karmas as they experience those bumps and thus be that much lighter when they finally reach 5D Earth.

Children and Grandchildren

We are sometimes asked about how young children can make this major transition to the 5D New Earth. It is important to understand that many young children are naturally suited to the 5D realms, particularly if they make the transition before they start using mobile phones! They will not have to make many adjustments themselves and they will try to get their parents to wake up sufficiently for them to move up also. Unfortunately, their parents do not always listen to their children.

If you have a child, it's like with any friend, you find ways and situations when you can quietly share with them the truths about what's coming. The child then has the choice as to what extent to respond.

You can put your child in their own sphere and take responsibility for maintaining it each day. This can gradually be shared with the child as they grow older so they interact directly with their own sphere and eventually take full responsibility for it. A family can set up their spheres so all interconnect with each other, with one main connection for the whole family to the Central Sphere.

A similar approach can be made by grandparents for their grandchildren, if the parents are not awake and participating. You do not need to have concerns that you are exceeding your authority or your rights as a grandparent. You are ultimately individuals who have karmic connections with the young child, whether they are a grandchild or you are taking care of them. You put out your energy and you share your truth.

That is the true meaning of life here, you share what is real for you. Hopefully this is of a somewhat loving and joyful quality but that is not true for everybody, as you know. For the Dnet participant, however, sharing your truth is a delight for the other person, of whatever age.

The Souls who do not Qualify for Ascension

When a Soul incarnated after choosing the parents, the nation, the time period and the Life Destiny Pattern, they knew what the possibilities and probabilities were looking like in terms of being part of the Ascension to 5D. Many of their Higher Selves chose well but some did not make their estimates and projections as well as they thought they had done.

But that is part of the evolutionary experience – being a Soul, you take your chances. You know that your Higher Self is doing its best to provide you with an evolutionary pattern which is going to work. Sometimes they do, sometimes they do not. Within that, even if an evolutionary pattern worked out as intended, it may be that the individual Soul needs more lifetimes at 3D and 4D levels. Right now, many Souls are being advised to connect with the Dnet as a great aid to getting back onto their higher evolutionary Path, stepping out of the consequences of unwise choices earlier in their lives.

Dnet is Open to all with Sufficient Strength of Mind and Will

As part of being members of this amazing new energy of the Dnet, we are asking some things of you in return, particularly within the arena of "service to others", which is, of course, a key part of the 5D curriculum. This form of service needs to be as automatic as serving yourself and your family.

Within this service orientation, there is a tremendous need to find your own personal way in which to explain to others about this opportunity of the Dnet. Each of you has your own way of sharing good news. This is not the same as selling a product or service, although some of you are good at that anyway. Enthusiasm is often the very best way to draw people in.

The Dnet is not an exclusive society in any way at all. It is open to any individual who has the strength of mind and the will to step through an open doorway into a new state of being. But we do not underestimate the weight that people carry or are pulling behind them which can, if not addressed, get in the way of any new step and even pull an individual backwards at the very moment when they need to move forwards in strength.

CHAPTER TEN
Joining the Dnet, An Invitation

During the next few months, specific events and sights will make it very clear that it's "all change" with life on Earth as we know it. This will be more a release and conclusion to the malfunctioning and distorted old third dimensional (3D) world, rather than specific disasters. Plate movements and their associated tremors will no doubt continue.

The challenge for those wishing to be part of the 5D New Earth is to align themselves with a specific energy structure which will, day by day, draw them inexorably towards that New World. The rampant negativity on 3D Earth has unfortunately got in the way, to some extent, of even the most determined individuals moving forward towards the Light. While they may have achieved a Consciousness significantly beyond the mainstream muddle and chaos, the yawning gap between their current level of Being and even the most simple manifestation of the 5D New Earth is still very substantial.

This is not in any way any kind of judgement on the Spiritual seekers, who have often moved forwards against extraordinary opposition and whose sense of will has been exercised to the full. We mention it as part of a clear description of the current situation with even the more awakened and Spiritually-inclined members of humanity, while being an accurate measure of the immcdiate challenge for an individual to Ascend to 5D over the few remaining months.

The Dnet is a Powerful Energy Structure

To meet this vital need to bridge this energetic gap, the Spiritual Hierarchy (and Quan Yin in particular) is offering each aspiring individual the immediate opportunity to join the Fifth Dimensional Network (Dnet). This is a powerful energy structure specifically designed to provide a safe and powerful transition to the 5D New Earth. It offers both protection from less than powerful influences along with a loving inspiration to enable the mind, body and Spirit of each individual to develop the refined vibrations necessary to graduate to the New Earth as Gaia makes her final move upwards to complete her Ascension.

In the next section, we set out the detailed benefits and requirements of joining and operating within the Dnet.

Why Join the Dnet?

1. Because it's real and offers you opportunities that have previously only been open to people who have spent their entire life in a temple. It's simple and practical and you do not need to devote each and every day to it.

2. Those individuals who have gone deeply into the Dnet cannot even begin to describe how wonderful it is and, indeed, what a privilege. They could not imagine going back to their prior situations. That would be like suddenly becoming blind, deaf and dumb by comparison.

3. You will have direct access to a multitude of Spiritual Masters and other Light energies.

4. Energy will be continually fed into you and this gradually enhances all of your higher functions:

    i. Your powers to heal others will increase considerably.

    ii. Spiritual contact will become far more effective and much clearer.

    iii. Your chakras will open fully due to the raised energy levels.

    iv. You will start seeing much more on many planes.

    v. Your inner knowingness will increase.

    vi. You will be able to link up with another Dnet member anywhere in the world.

vii. Some will be able to predict future events.

viii. Some will become much more aware of past lives.

ix. And much more.

5. The raised energy levels will also benefit you physically as it is like having daily healing sessions on yourself:

   i. You will be able to consciously move energy to any part of your body for healing.

   ii. Gradually the incoming Dnet energy will break down blockages in your body, allowing it to flow more freely throughout.

   iii. You will feel energized.

   iv. You will look and feel younger.

   v. You will rarely be ill.

   vi. You will become stronger all round.

6. You will become part of a family of like minded people.

7. You will be protected from bugs and attachments. Everyone in the Dnet is automatically cleared twice a day, in case any get through.

8. The major goal of the Dnet is to give you direct access to the 5D energy and, as your energy levels increase, so this will start to be fed into your Spirit and body. This 5D energy is incredible and unlike anything you will have experienced. It will change you fundamentally and move you forward in ways you cannot imagine. It is a bridge between our lives in this World and the Living Spirit throughout the Universe.

Why might you choose Not to Join? Nothing worth having is without Effort.

1. You have to spend 10 minutes a day reinforcing your connection to it. Anyone who is not prepared to do that simply doesn't qualify to be part of it.

2. Once you advance Spiritually, you become a potential target for bugs or attachments. Anyone who is Spiritually aware is a target anyway but, the more you advance, the more attractive you become. This has always been true for seekers on the Path.

3. You will change as a person as your vibration rises and as you experience and understand more. Some people may think you are going peculiar. It will be hard to share many of your new experiences with those close to you and this will probably put a strain on friendships and relationships. Others may resent what is happening to you, unless they also want to advance Spiritually..

4. It can be quite demanding at first because so much is being changed in you spiritually and physically and you may be quite tired sometimes. But it passes.

Each reader is sincerely invited to join this special Network by following the 11 step instructions set out in Chapter Ten. The procedure is straightforward and connection can be accomplished through a meditative focus and simple visualisation of just five minutes in the morning – the same in the evening. A support team is available (Contact Us) should you find that questions come up or difficulties arise, with which you need help.

CHAPTER ELEVEN
The Eleven Steps to Joining the Dnet

Joining this network will provide you with the energy and support structure that you need to go to Fifth Dimensional (5D) Consciousness, as the Earth completes her Ascension. It will also enable you to protect yourself as you evolve individually. It directly connects people, who wish to advance, with the energies of the Light: Archangels, Spiritual Masters, Gaia (the Spirit of our planet) and many other Higher Beings.

In times past, the Dnet might have been described as a "Gift from God", which it is, but we are going to focus here on its practical aspects as a tool for those seeking to work constructively with cosmic energy. The Dnet is centred on a protective Central Sphere created by specific energies of the Light, attuned so that they can interact fully with us.

As the Dnet grows, it is becoming a living network with a powerful Centre connected to an extensive web of individual domes. Power comes from the Central Sphere and spreads out to anyone in the Dnet but, in addition, it is growing to be large enough to generate lateral energy across the Dnet. The Dnet is open to anyone wishing to join who wants to work with the Light and, within that condition, everyone is welcome.

Getting Started with your Own Sphere

1. Create/visualise the sphere of loving light energy around you, ask it to protect you against bugs, harmful and unwanted attachments or entities, but to allow in freely the good energies of the Light.

2. Then ask the sphere to make an outer shell diamond-hard, visualize fire all around the outside of it.

3. Create a shaft of energy passing through your Heart Centre and extending out to the shell of the sphere, in front of you and also to the rear.

4. Create a second shaft of energy passing sideways through your heart centre, extending to the shell of the sphere to your left and similarly to your right.

5. Create a third shaft of energy passing vertically through your heart centre, extending to the shell of the sphere above you and similarly below you, completing a three dimensional cross inside the sphere centred on your heart centre and extending out to the shell of the sphere.

6. Ask the sphere energy to make the shell impervious to bugs, harmful and unwanted attachments but to stay open to the flow of good energies of the Light.

7. Visualize an inner sphere shell about 20% of the way inside the outer sphere and ask the energy to make the inner sphere shell also impervious to bugs, harmful and unwanted attachments, while being completely open to the good energies of the Light. Thank the loving Light energy.

8. Ask Gaia to open up her energy inside you and the sphere and then thank her.

9. Invite Yin (a black devic energy) to also open up inside you and your sphere and thank it.

10. Ask Yang (a red devic energy) to also open up inside you and your sphere and thank it.

11. With each of these energies, bring it into being and simply overlay one on top of another. Once you have joined with everything, picture the sphere filled with bright golden white light.

Second Stage: Joining on to the Central Sphere

Practice using your personal protective sphere for a few days or weeks, learning to strengthen and reinforce it by tuning in for a few minutes in the morning and a few minutes similarly in the evening. When you feel comfortable with your sphere, you are invited to connect up with the Central Sphere and the full Fifth Dimensional Network.

To join with this central sphere visualize a tube or shaft extending from your outer shell all the way out to the Central Sphere and joining its outer shell. State that only the good energies of the Light are allowed into the tube and that only they can travel between the two spheres and enter yours. Imagine the tube full of white loving energy flowing into your sphere from the central sphere but stipulating "not the other way".

This procedure has been designed so that you can do it yourself, but should you have any doubts or concerns feel free to email us at: keith@fifthdimensionalnetwork.com and ask to be joined to the Central Sphere and, if you wish, to be fully energised at the 5D level. The support team will respond.

Third Stage: Connecting to the full Fifth Dimensional Energy and Network

The 5D energy was quite recently made available to the Dnet when we helped to convert a portal, that had delivered earth energy for centuries, into a direct shaft of connection to the 5D energy of the New Earth. The link was simultaneously formed inside the Central Sphere of the Network. To connect up to the 5D energy, come to a day workshop if at all possible. Alternatively, just open yourself to the 5D energy and it will flow in and around you, just like the other energies from the Central Sphere. Feel free to contact the support team at the above email address.

If you wish to join with the sphere of someone else in the Dnet, then first you must have their permission and they must also visualize you connecting with their sphere. Then join their sphere with yours in the same way as for connecting with the Central Sphere. This would be most appropriate for close family members or close friends.

If you then allow others to join with your own sphere, ensure that their protective sphere is constructed the same way as yours and that the tube or shaft connects between your spheres in the same way as to the Central Sphere. Allow the energy to flow into their sphere. It will be compensated for by drawing more power from the Central Sphere. State clearly and bring into being the absolute condition that only the good energies of the Light are allowed into the tube at all times and that only they can travel between the spheres.

When you are comfortable with the connection between the individual spheres, the energy will flow both ways. You can join with as many other individual spheres as you wish, but one sphere is sufficient, as they are becoming one fully integrated network. Only allow connections that you want.

If you subsequently want to disconnect from another sphere, then simply visualize the connection vanishing and state that no connection is henceforth allowed with that other sphere, unless the shaft is formally re-instated with your explicit consent. Similarly, should you wish to leave the Dnet and take down your own protective sphere, simply visualize it disappearing.

This is very much about your ability and determination to visualize these things and/or will them into being. Please make sure you do the practice twice a day, so both the image and the actual energy structure become stronger and more powerful.

Remember this is basically a community of people who want to work with the Light and advance to 5D, joining with the energies of the Light that can help them. We are all equal in this endeavour and nobody wants anything from anyone else. We only want to help others to help themselves.

CHAPTER TWELVE
Dealing with Attachments, Entities and Bugs

Spiritual advancement is wonderful in so many ways and sometimes the feeling is incredible when joining with energies of the Light. But, like all good things in life, it comes at a price and there are opposing forces that may seek to undermine or attack a student on the Path. These are commonly known as attachments, entities or bugs — sometimes confused with evil spirits, ghosts or poltergeists.

In Western society, we generally regard such things as imagination, depression, mental health problems or even insanity. The institutional response is pills, more pills and even being locked up. In some places in the East, there is a greater awareness of such things and some organisations are able to deal with the attachments and entities. Most of the main religions consider them to be evil demons or spirits and treat them as such, attempting to exorcise them within the values of their particular religion. However, a few religions and Spiritual groups accept that attachments exist and choose to address them, both esoterically and practically.

Most people in the mainstream West reading about all this would find it hard to believe. They further might think that even discussing this was an indication of mental instability or worse. Most of those same people would have the same lack of understanding about the existence of spirits, angels, guides, Spiritual advancement and maybe even God. Those of us brought up on a diet of "blind science" went through an often long unawareness, until one day wisdom began to dawn.

Understanding these Life Forms

This message, however, is directed at people who are sufficiently aware that such things at least may exist. It is especially relevant to those who are advancing Spiritually and/or who feel they may have such an attachment on them already.

These attachments/entities/bugs are life forms that can move between dimensions and there are many types of them. Only some use hosts to supply them with energy, much like on Earth a few species like mosquitoes and leeches feed on human blood. Some are more powerful than others, some are more intelligent and overall there is quite a variation in their characteristics.. They are no more evil than are leeches or mosquitoes but they are clearly our enemies. We shall refer to them as "bugs" for short, since that is effectively how they operate.

Once they land on a host, it takes them a little while to become established — much like a plant takes root before growing. Because of this, they usually have little impact at first. But, over time, they become established in the body and start to make more demands of it. They link into the energetic system of the host: favourite places including the womb, the area around the stomach, the base of the back and even the head. As they become firmly established, so they draw an ever increasing amount of energy from the host, who becomes progressively weaker.

Most people in this situation sense that something is wrong but they do not understand what is going on. They may grow progressively more tired, run down, irritable, nervous, introspective, irrational, afraid to go out of their homes and less able to work or focus properly. They may hear voices in their heads, feel like something is inside of them, become paranoid, and even suicidal. Worst of all, people tell them it is all in their imagination, so they feel they are losing their grip on reality.

Of course, these symptoms can also exist in people with more physical illnesses and I am absolutely not saying that everyone with those symptoms has a bug on them. Nor would someone with a bug necessarily show all of these symptoms, as it varies enormously with the person and the bug. Some of them are terrible and devastate your life, whilst others are fairly unobtrusive and are "bearable", while still being undesirable. Then some people are innately more sensitive to them compared with others who are largely oblivious.

Removing Bugs and Establishing Protection

It is likely that millions of people around the world have bugs on them. They certainly are not rare. We have been able to help people who have been treated unsuccessfully over long periods by doctors and psychiatrists with assorted drugs. The good news is that they have been cured of their condition in less than 20 minutes, often without any direct communication with them and only in rare cases actually seeing them face to face.

So why do some people get the bugs and not others? The bugs are attracted to vitality and/or the beginnings of a higher consciousness – there is just more energy for them to feed off. Fortunately, some people have some natural protection which reduces their availability.

The aura normally gives us some protection from bugs but, when you grow Spiritually, it can be ruptured temporarily and they can get through. But with Spiritual consciousness comes an ability to form a special protective sphere (like in the Fifth Dimensional Network (Dnet)) that keeps them out, so long as the individual maintains their daily routine of energetic protection.

Some people are born with or develop defective auras and some of these people can carry bugs for years, which blight their lives. Other people damage their own auras with things like excessive drink or drugs (all sorts) — accidents and other shocks can also affect them.

People who are involved in healing: Reiki, yoga, meditation etc can also experience their Spiritual growth causing some disturbance of the aura.

Whatever the cause or prior conditions, their elevated energy makes them desirable hosts and are more visible to the bugs. The greater the energy, the more desirable is the host. When teachers show people how to protect themselves, there is little or no problem. However, many teachers do not have a clue about the bugs and simply don't know how protection can be created, let alone maintained consistently. People with exceptionally high levels of energy are prime targets but their personal protection can also be stronger, provided they use a sound approach. There is certainly nothing to fear in dealing with the bugs except extreme apathy.

Many ordinary people recently have started advancing Spiritually because the Earth herself is Ascending. We all depend upon the energy from the Earth to sustain us in much the same way we need to breathe air and to eat food. Once her energy has shifted, people who haven't advanced will find it increasingly difficult to absorb that energy and to function in a straightforward way. Many Spirit guides and teachers are converging on the Earth to help with this transition and they are making it much easier to advance. However, the bugs also know what is happening and they do not want any higher consciousness, so they are gathering in strength to take advantage of people who may be vulnerable, because of the changes through which they are going.

Most of these people will have no knowledge or understanding of what is happening to them Spiritually and, once they become hosts, many will be lost to further advance unless helped. The Dnet enables the liberation and protection of large numbers of people. Our support team have all personally experienced bugs of different varieties first hand so can deal effectively with helping and counselling people before and after the intervention.

The Good News is that if any person already has a bug on them, it will be automatically removed on joining the Dnet.

Dealing with Attachments, Entities and Bugs

There are various approaches to teaching people how to develop their own protection and some are better than others. Our way is for each individual to develop a protective sphere within a preformed network and that is explained in detail in Chapter Eleven. We are recommending this approach on the basis that it works well and is easy to maintain, taking only 10 minutes a day. We do not operate on a religious basis – that is obviously for each person to decide about for themselves, although most of us do believe in various aspects of God.

We cannot set up a protective sphere for an individual without the permission of that person, unless that individual is a young child or is otherwise unable to make such a decision for themselves. Please do not abuse this as your own good wishes for someone else may be not for their Highest Good, however well-intentioned. If you have questions on any of this or need help, please contact us through our website: www.fifthdimensionalnetwork.com.

CHAPTER THIRTEEN
How Best to Work with the Dnet

The Dnet structure is specifically designed to enable its participants to readily progress to 5D Consciousness and the Dnet can provide you with the facilities to achieve it. Given the Earth's decision to Ascend herself, ideally we should all have been preparing for the transition to 5D for the last decade or two. However, most of us have left it somewhat late and now need to put in more effort in order to be ready on time.

Many high energies have come together (the Management Team) to design the 5D energy structure and bring it into being. Once this had been accomplished, a direct link to the 5D New Earth was established accessible from inside the Dnet. This energy is available to anyone who is ready and asks specifically for it.

People will also be able to work between dimensions as that facility is also available to people in the Dnet and can be taught to anyone who wants it. This was necessary for the forging of a direct link to the 5D. You also have direct access to many higher beings, energies and guides to an extent that is impossible for most people. Your existing connections will be amplified and strengthened.

Automatic Clearance

Every participant within the Dnet (and their protective sphere) is automatically cleared of any and all external negativity twice a day so, if a bug does get through your defences, you know it will not be there for long. If you cannot wait that long then contact one of us and if possible, you will be cleared sooner. Through the website you can share your experiences since joining the Dnet (for greater learning) and also ask to connect with others in the network who wish to share in similar fashion. In this way, local or regional groups can be formed, if people wish to take the initiative.

The Dnet does not in any way prevent you from working with your current teachers, guides, doorkeepers or anyone else that you choose to be involved with. Indeed, many of them may be working within it anyway and you can open yourself to a broader range of energy. The Dnet does not control you or your life in any way whatsoever but merely acts as a tool for enlightenment and a safety net that you may or may not choose to utilise.

Self-Regulating Energy Levels

The Dnet is automatically regulating as the Management Team will feed you with a level of energy that you can sustain. They will also increase the level if you need extra for something like healing. You can greatly help that process by indicating what level you normally want. So if you call your current level 20, double it every week so it will be 40 next week, 80 the week after, 160 the following week etc. Don't try to go slower or faster as it won't do you any good and may confuse the Team.

When you connect, ask for the desired level you want: for example, if you want 320, you ask for 320 plus meaning that the Team are free to increase or moderate the level in my sphere as appropriate. This will give the Team a feel for what you need and they will know to increase it for healing or for any other activity.

Gaia, the loving Light energy, along with the black and red devic energies of Yin and Yang, are all present with the Ascended Masters and Archangels in the Dnet Central Sphere. The reason you connect your own individual sphere to them as well is so these energies can then reach you both directly and indirectly through the Dnet connection..

More Power and Vitality

The energies in the Dnet are not the same as vitality. For example, when you heal someone, you usually connect with guides and other wonderful energies and, whilst they may feel really nice at the time, they rarely fill you with vitality during the following day. But all people absorb energy from their surroundings and particularly from the Yin and Yang devic energies, red and black. It is these energies that give you more vitality and, by attunement, you can learn to draw more from them.

Remember all of these energies are alive and vastly more intelligent than us, so always be respectful saying "please" and "thanks". It is just good manners but it helps to sustain balance between the realms.

The Dnet gives you more personal power and, used correctly over time, this translates into more vitality. A child has boundless energy because all his energy routes and gates are wide open so he draws in energy like a sponge. As we age, the routes partially block like furred arteries and the gates no longer open properly or just stay partly open. Either way, we pull in less and less energy in consequence. We also become unbalanced energetically and Spiritually so we grow progressively wearier.

The Dnet suddenly increases the energy going into you and this enables you to use potential gifts that weren't available to you before because you could not power them — much like you cannot power headlights off a flat battery. So your chakras are able to open, you can use your third eye, your healing becomes far more powerful, you can easily heal people in remote locations.

In martial arts, we can hurl people across the room with our index fingers or we can ward off strikes without even touching our opponents and so on. But, if you don't run regularly yet choose to set off on a 5 mile run because you suddenly have the energy for it, your body will ache for days afterwards because your organs and limbs aren't used to it. In other words, there is a need for consistency in your rejuvenation.

You will have to be rewired physically and Spiritually both to handle the extra energy and ultimately to make the move to 5D. These changes will automatically happen in stages and they will leave you tired at times, just as will using your new gifts. Between the stages you will feel really good.

Energy flows around the body through known routes and there are main and secondary gates along these routes. A young person will have little difficulty adapting to the new energy source because the routes and gates will function perfectly so the increased energy will flow freely. Others will have partial and total blockages in some routes while some gates will not open and close freely. This did not matter with the normal energy flow but now it will show up in discomfort or even some pain in those areas.

The Dnet energy will try to break down the blockages and the body will try to fix the gates and there will be an all round improvement in your health but it takes time. The physical changes will be easier for people who do Tai Chi, Chi Kung or yoga, while meditation will help with the Spiritual changes. We can help with this by advising on how to clear yourself more quickly and will recommend some easy exercises.

You will acquire new gifts or, in reality, you will activate or enhance gifts that are already inside you but were not being powered up because there was not enough energy available or because the routes were partially or totally blocked. This means you will start seeing, sensing and hearing things that some people around you cannot. Spirits may become attracted to you because they will see the changes in your auras it expands and becomes fuller.

Psychic Opening

It is possible that you may start seeing more of your past lives, you may receive visions of future events, and some will become able to use telepathy. There are now people in the Dnet who can use these and many other advanced skills. Many of them had never been able to do anything out of the ordinary before joining.

If it all sounds too good to be true, then think again. Many of your family and friends will think you are becoming unhinged and you will likely find yourself drifting away from them to new friends. A part of you will be desperate to take your family and old friends with you on this journey but they will most likely think that you have lost the plot, to a greater or lesser extent. Sensing what other people feel about you isn't always that great either and seeing things that you have never seen before takes some getting used to.

Then, as we discuss in Chapter Twelve "Attachments and Bugs", there are the bugs and that is the toughest thing of all to deal with. But the Dnet will shelter you from most of them and the other members will help by sharing their experiences. Once you have learned you can beat them, they just become an occasional pain in the arse like mosquitoes. Unfortunately, many people in mainstream life walk around with them all the time, without any knowledge of their presence. However, through using the Dnet you will have complete protection and balance, which will see you through any situation.

If people do not want to work with the Light, they will not be allowed to connect and, in any case, the energy would be unpalatable for them. Everyone is equal and has the same right of access to the energies. It's nothing to do with your background. As more join, the Network will grow and become stronger and more energies will join to help. Many of those who join early will help those who join later and hopefully it will become like an extended family.

CHAPTER FOURTEEN
5D Energy and the Dnet,
A Personal Perspective

I would like to be able to say more than I will about this but the simple fact is that it is still new to me as well. Until twelve years ago, I had no Spiritual gifts whatsoever, and only believed in science, so it has been a hard road for me, but now I have been lent many gifts. I emphasise "lent" because they have shown me they can easily take them away and I am left with just me!

I am learning and being taught how to work with it on a daily basis. So I will explain what I can and, as I learn more, I will pass that on and hopefully others will also relay and share their experiences of the Dnet.

The Energies of the Dnet

In this chapter and in various articles, I often refer to "they" or the "energies". I am working with a considerable number of different energies and entities from the Light, including Spiritual Masters and Archangels. I have been taught for some time by a Tai Chi archetype and a healing archetype.

I also work with some specialised guides so, whenever I say "they" or the energies, I am referring to this Management Team, comprising one or more of the above. I don't want to sound flash over this because I feel just like a modest grain of sand in comparison to any of them. Some other people communicate with them far better than I can.

Also, anyone in the Dnet has the same right of access to any of them as me as they learn to tune in. I have been just as much out of my depth as anyone else and much of it is beyond mental understanding. So I do my best to help pass on the guidance to you and, in turn, I hope others will help in a similar manner.

Working with the 5D Energies

The 5D energy opened in the main sphere when the Team converted the Somerset energy portal into a connection or portal to the 5D. What I did not realize at the time was that, as we helped with this process, they also opened the same 5D portal inside the main sphere, so it simultaneously exists in both places. This of course, isn't possible in our 3D world and indeed, the sphere also doesn't actually exist in our "normal" reality. Yet the existence of your sphere, connected to the 5D reality, will positively change your 3D existence.

I work with many portals both opening them and clearing them of bugs. They all feel similar with beautiful and powerful light energy streaming out. The 5D portal feels completely different and looks almost like a black hole and can feel cold and empty like space. That's why we visualize it as a black core in the connecting tube. Yet the energy emanates in many different forms (most of which I am not able to see or understand at present) and is indeed very beautiful. It also joins with the other energies in the sphere to produce a very powerful and unique energy signature.

So I see it as a black energy sometimes and other times as a bright energy or as a black energy inside a light energy. But I feel that there are many more colours to it and it exists in forms that I cannot see or sense or even comprehend. The energy isn't to be confused with energies of the dark side as it is black in colour only and you will learn to see other colours in and around it.

The energy delivered to everyone in the Dnet is automatically adjusted to a level that each person can utilize and increases over time as their abilities increase. This is true of all the types of energy flowing, including that of 5D, so currently the levels available to most people are quite modest.

I am more closely connected to the 5D energy than anyone else in the Dnet since I have been used in its manifestation. I normally work at a higher energy level with the other energies both Spiritually and physically and they have been preparing me to do this. Yet I am only able to handle the 5D energy at a modest level. Even then it makes my body shake when I even slightly increase it. Not in an unpleasant way and it does pass, but it feels so different to any other energy I have ever experienced.

Many people say they are already living a 5D life and, whilst it may be true for some of them, many may be quite mistaken. The reason I question whether or not people are already living a 5D life is because the 5D energy is extremely difficult to work with, while still living on planet Earth (before her Ascension). So living inside it would be next to impossible currently. Whilst some people may be living their lives with many of the qualities required for 5D living, this is not the same as actually living a 5D life. But whatever level you are at, the Dnet will enable you to progress and ultimately be ready for the transition to full 5D.

Working with the Spiritual Management Team

The Management Team have begun to show two of us how to bring it into our bodies and use it physically, both on its own and in combination with other energies. We both do Tai Chi and Chi Kung and other related activates. We have spent a long time opening up the channels and gates in our body, while practising moving and using different energies both individually and in different combinations. We have been taught how to move the energies outside of our bodies between dimensions and can work from here on ourselves or others Spiritually or physically. In this way, we use it to clear bugs and attachments from people — also to cleanse and heal specific places.

These are not our gifts but are loans from the Team and they can and do cut them off at any time and, when they are taken off us, we feel incredibly vulnerable, weak and empty. It is good to be reminded from time to time as it teaches you that you are very minor by comparison and that you greatly value the loans.

When we work with a more typical energy of the Light, we feel buoyed up and very powerful. Some of them are so loving that a feeling of warmth overwhelms you. The dimensional energies and entities we work with are different, they are more like black energies and feel cold yet warm simultaneously, empty yet still pleasant like the 5D energy. We work closely with these in conjunction with other energies of the Light when we are clearing bugs, as we move them into different dimensions.

The single biggest mistake that people and especially religious representatives make is to only offer the bugs death — so of course they fight hard. With us, they know the game is up. If they stay they will die so they naturally take the escape route we offer them to go to another far away dimension. Their return is blocked because we close that dimensional gate behind them — it is a one-way route.

The other energies of the Light strengthen us in different ways and we feel the strength in each other. That strength may be physical, giving us great power, or it may be Spiritual enabling us to heal or to clear bugs. But these extra vibrational energies give us physical strength. They also weaken our opponent and destabilise them. We feel it in the other person and, ironically, it makes us feel very vulnerable.

It also increases our Spiritual abilities as a bridge is formed between our normal world and the other dimensions where we use our other abilities such as the third eye. When used in conjunction with the other energies, you have a great power source for the chakras and, suddenly, they all light up like a Christmas tree.

I have found that some of my chakras are partially blocked (something I never even knew before) plus they extend out far beyond anything I imagined. I can now feel them on my back as well and can feel the energy flowing through. Working with the 5D energy, in terms of power output, is like working with a nuclear reactor compared with a steam engine!

I have been asked why a large number of energies are working with the Dnet as a Team, rather than just one like Quan Yin, who originally created it. I believe it is because they all simultaneously perform other tasks as well and each has a certain role to play in the Dnet Team and brings different gifts to the operation. The Dnet is stronger for that and needs to be as it will be tested by the dark forces (like everything else on the current Earthplane) who do not want the changes. The dimensional energies are but one example of how they can perform some tasks better than say the guides etc.

Internalising the New Energies

The 5D energy has only been added very recently and, whilst other energies of the Light are still joining, many others had to be in place before the 5D energy could be sustained in the Dnet. It is currently only generating a tiny fraction of its capacity because nobody is able to use more of it.

Initially, just like the other energies, it will gradually and lovingly seep into your individual Spirit and your body, while increasing as quickly as you can adapt to it. Before you can absorb very much of it, you will need to greatly increase the intensity of the other energies in you, to literally "quicken" yourself. Without them, you could not handle the 5D energy.

This will all happen naturally through being plugged into the Central Sphere of the Dnet. You will hardly notice the growing intensity or the more refined Attunement at first although, as they accumulate, you will be more and more affected by them.

I have begun the process of assimilating the 5D energy into my body as well as my Spirit and it isn't easy. I visualize it filling up my body and try to keep that image when working with it and the other energies. It becomes easier with practice, just like developing any other new skill was difficult at first.

The energy of the Dnet is inside me, as it is with all the people in the Dnet, who are connected to it. This flows through me, healing and clearing people and places. So far I can only handle tiny levels of it and it is only growing inside me at the rate I can handle physically and spiritually. I work between dimensions, with guides and the 5D energy is flowing through me and I heal and clear people and places

This opportunity is open to anyone who has the ability and heart to connect to it and wants to work with the Light. If they let someone like me (in my original state) join in , then anyone can as long as they want to lead a good life, regardless of any mistakes they may have made in this life. I have made many and I try to make up for past mistakes.

I am still learning how to work with all these energies and the structures available and I will have to keep updating this on a continual basis. Even in the last week, my understanding of 5D has increased significantly. I sense and know that there is a long way to go yet, for everybody operating with the Dnet.

Personally though, I would absolutely hate to go back to what I was as it would be like becoming blind, deaf and dumb all at once. I have had some beautiful experiences with this and every day is a wonderful adventure. I have bathed in the new 5D energy and it is lovely. Some of the energies I have joined with have been a total joy and I regard this as an honour.

Keith Laidler

CHAPTER FIFTEEN
Helping Others Share in the Dnet

Once you are settled properly into the Dnet, you will know at a deep inner level that it is the right thing to go. It's an amazingly ingenious concept and you will be able to feel it working. You will derive many benefits from it and you will steadily move towards 5D Consciousness.

Well, that's wonderful for us individually but what about everyone else? How do we help them? How do we convince our friends and families that this is all real and not just some elaborate fantasy? Why should they believe that this is any different from memories of other Spiritual imaginings that did not come about?

Choosing Suitable People to Invite

Fortunately, you do not have to do any such "convincing" and all you actually need to do is to try to help two other people to join. Naturally, you choose to approach those people you know who are likely to be most open to a new creation like the Dnet. These may be individuals who have already spent part of their lives searching for meaning beyond the material and/or are seeking to engage with energies beyond the physical.

This may not even necessarily include your family or friends unless they qualify in terms of their aspirations outlined above. In truth, many people are not ready, able or willing to make the journey and it is certainly not for us to decide what is best for them. It's usually a big enough struggle trying to find the correct route in life for ourselves! You will know the people who can and want to join because you will feel it and you will be guided if you open yourselves to that.

A Wonderful Framework for a Finer Way of Living

The Dnet is not a religion and we certainly are not here to ram our beliefs down the throat of anyone who happens to be nearby. Nor do we want people to join purely as an act of faith, or just to please somebody else. The Dnet is real and when you join it you will know it and you will be affected by it both Spiritually and physically. Many of you will use the energy to heal people and your friends will notice a sense of "upgrade" in you, without being able to put their fingers on what exactly has changed.

It is a unique energy structure offering multiple benefits and that is why people will not only join but will go deeper into it, encouraging others to join also. Those who would benefit from joining will sense a different kind of energy in you – an extra buoyancy perhaps. You can offer them help and introduce them to the first stages of the Dnet and then simply leave it up to them. If they are ready and able, then they will join and, if not, they will choose otherwise.

Some will be able to help many join, others only one or two and maybe some none. It is not critical as the Dnet is mostly for you but it will be nice if you can try to help others experience it too and, if we can all average helping two people to join, then the total number of participants will grow very quickly.

Far from being associated with any kind of prediction of "doom" or catastrophe, the Dnet is a wonderful living framework and something we have all been yearning and striving for over many lifetimes. We finally get to break the shackles of a 3D existence and move into far more pleasant and fulfilling ways of living. That is also true for other inhabitants of this planet and Gaia herself. It may be a challenging transition but most good things are like that.

The most difficult part of this for almost all of us concerns our families and close friends. I am sure we will try to introduce them to this path, giving them the details of the Dnet website so they can learn about it for themselves, as that will make it a lot easier to explain and help open the door.

Nonetheless, many people will feel sorry for us and have concerns about our sanity and we just have to accept it. Maybe they won't want to make the journey with us or they won't be ready or capable. Either way, we have to accept their reality as it is. All we can do is to make the offer and to keep it open.

This human life passes quickly and soon we will inevitably part from our families anyway. In most cases, if they were able to understand the value of what is available, they would not want us to be held back and to undergo more 3D lives. We have never said that this is an easy route and it is not.

The Dnet and the Earth Changes

We are not suggesting that by joining the Dnet you will in some way avoid the coming changes on 3D Earth. Even though most people will choose to stay at the 3D level as is their right, you as an evolving individual have every right to move to the 5D level. One way or the other, we will still part from our families and friends at some point anyway, so we may as well go to 5D, while the door is open. It's a lot easier to say or write this than to do it in practice, yet the choice is a serious one which we must all make.

As things deteriorate and people look for Spiritual homes or other options, then we can help more of these individuals — some previously sceptical people may be won over. With each passing month, the transition to 5D will become harder simply because there will be less time in which to make the transition but we need to be ready and able to help any latecomers anyway.

Think of the Dnet as a passenger jet where we offer people the opportunity of a free flight and we even offer to help them to the airport. But we cannot force them to go and we may not even get them to understand why we want to go at all, let alone where we are going to. Remember you join the Dnet so you are able to choose to make the transition when the time comes. Yet you can still elect to leave it and stay in 3D. But you cannot leave joining it until the last minute and then decide you want to go to 5D, as if by waving a magic wand. There's plenty of magic here but it needs some weeks and months to experience it for yourself and deeply attune to the much higher vibrations of 5D Consciousness.

FURTHER RESOURCES AND CONTACT INFORMATION

Websites

Our website:
www.fifthdimensionalnetwork.com

For the background to 2012:
www.revolutionof2012.net

For news about Earth Changes:
www.zetatalk.com

Publications

"The Revolution of 2012, Volume One: The Preparation"
by Andrew Smith

"The Revolution of 2012, Volume Two: The Challenge"
by Andrew Smith

"The Revolution of 2012, Volume Three: Taking Action"
by Andrew Smith

"Angels of the Cosmos"
by Masao Murata (Byakko Press)

Contact the Authors

Email for Keith Laidler: keith@fifthdimensionalnetwork.com

Email for Andrew Smith: info@fifthdimensionalnetwork.com